T0286933

VUKOVICH

The Man Who Wouldn't Lift

Angelo Angelopolous

HALFCOURT PRESS
Indianapolis, IN

Vukovich: The Man Who Wouldn't Lift © 2024 Halfcourt Press

EAN-ISBN-13: 978-0-9987298-2-4

Cover designed by Phil Velikan

Printed in the United States of America
10 9 8 7 6 5 4 3 2

Distributed in the United States by Cardinal Publishers Group.
www.cardinalpub.com

Table of Contents

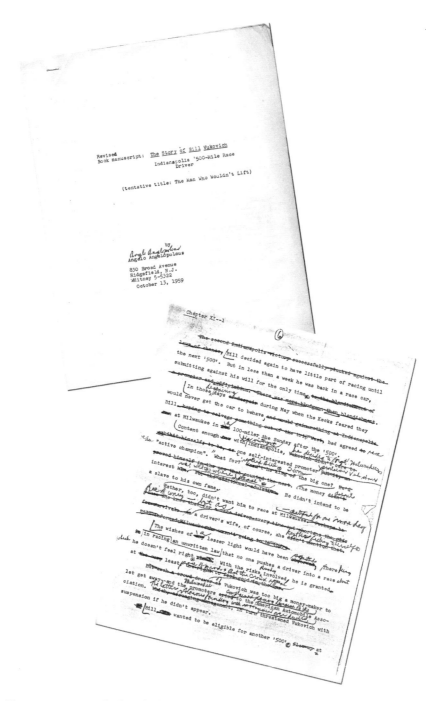

The cover page and a hand-edited inside page of Angelo Angelopolous' typewritten manuscript. He had a contract with a publisher to bring it out in 1960, but the project was abandoned for unknown reasons.

"He never met anybody who forgot about meeting him."

Prologue
By Mark Montieth

This book is a biography, according to literary classification. But it's also a drama, a mystery, and, ultimately, a tragedy. On multiple levels.

Angelo Angelopolous, one of the premier sportswriters of his era and a close friend of Bill Vukovich, labored over the manuscript throughout the final years of the fifties. He had a contract with an Indianapolis publishing firm, Bobbs Merrill, and two articles in *The Indianapolis News* announced a publication date of spring, 1960.

Why it was abandoned isn't clear. I talked with Angelo's wife, brother and a few close friends several years ago before I was aware of the manuscript's ongoing existence, and while some of them mentioned his attempt to publish a book none of them offered a reason for its demise.

Perhaps it couldn't be completed to Angelo's liking. The typewritten, double-spaced copy of the manuscript I received from his nephew Pete Kirles, who extracted it from a closet where it had been neglected for decades, was far from a finished work. Several sentences were rewritten by hand, sometimes illegibly. Entire paragraphs were crossed out, some of them worthy of restoration. Other copies of the manuscript had circulated through other hands, but none apparently was regarded as a final version, ready for publication, and at some point had presumably been discarded.

One theory, in my mind the best one, is that Angelo and Vukovich's widow, Esther, couldn't agree on some of the content. She obviously contributed to it, recounting details and conversations only she would have known. Perhaps they couldn't reach a consensus. Or, perhaps, there was disagreement over distribution of whatever profits might come from the book.

For whatever reason the project stalled, like a race car that blows an engine rounding out of the fourth turn and heading for the finish line. That mystery doesn't matter now, really. What's certain is that Angelo Angelopolous, same as Bill Vukovich, deserved a better fate. You'll read Vukovich's story in the following pages, but Angelo's needs to be told as well.

＊－＊

He was born in 1919, one of George and Helen Angelopolous' five children. He had three sisters and a younger brother, Jimmie. George Angelopolous had immigrated from Greece at age 16 and after settling in Indianapolis wound up owning and operating a successful grocery store on the city's near west side. The family lived above it.

Angelo was a senior member of Manual High School's city championship basketball team in 1936, but rarely played. His gift was writing about athletes, not being one. He began serious preparations for his newspaper career at Butler University, where, as a journalism major, he was editor of both the campus newspaper and yearbook. He also was president of his sophomore class, the Phi Delta Theta social fraternity, and the Butler chapter of the national Blue Key Honor Society, which recognizes students for leadership, academics, service, and character. Add to all that membership in the Utes Club, a sophomore men's society; the Sphinx Club, a junior men's honorary society; the Sigma Delta Chi national journalism society; the Kappa Tau Alpha national scholastic journalism honorary society; and the Sigma Tau Delta English honorary society.

In other words, not your typical college student.

The *News* hired him as a part-time correspondent to cover Butler athletic events during his senior year. He showed off his budding talent immediately. Writing a season preview for the 1939-40 basketball team, he referred to "the quest for the pot of goal at the end of hundreds of rainbow shots." He became a full-time staff member upon graduation.

Working for an afternoon newspaper, void of creativity-curtailing deadlines, enabled him to unleash his talent.

Just 18 months into his career, however, on infamous Dec. 7, 1941, Pearl Harbor was bombed. Angelo enlisted in the Navy the following month. The *News* ran a story on it, staging a photo that showed him sitting at a typewriter where he "pounded out his last yarn" before entering the service. Former Butler basketball star Bob Dietz, a close friend who also was enlisting, stood next to him, supposedly checking his work. The article reported they were "teamed up in one of the naval air units being prepared to let the Japs know the United States is intending to win this war."

Angelo breezed through flight training after which he served as an instructor for the advanced training squadrons in Texas and Florida for 22 months. He then was prepared for combat and deployed to the Pacific in January of 1945. He initially was a ferry pilot between the Philippines, Guam and the Midway atoll near the Hawaiian Islands and then assigned to the USS Hancock, from which he flew several missions over Japan.

Angelo was among the Hancock pilots who located prison camps, dropped supplies and medicine to troops and conducted inspections over bombed Japanese cities. One of those was Hiroshima, where the atom bomb was dropped on Aug. 6. Japan formally surrendered on Sept. 2. Angelo was discharged from the Navy in December and returned to his newspaper career in February. The *News* announced it under the headline, "And Now He's Back!"

He had entered the war talented, intelligent, handsome, and charismatic. Now he had the added sheen of a worldly war hero, too, adding a macho element to the mix. He seemed a "chosen one," perfectly fit for stardom, at least within the realm of a Midwestern sportswriter.

He wore his fame well, however. He had never been one to call attention to himself, by word or action. Although a prolific writer, he verbalized no more than necessary and when he did, he spoke quietly, barely above a whisper. He particularly didn't care to talk much about his war experiences. Still, that chapter of his life enhanced his image whether he liked it or not. He had visited more places and done more things and showed more courage than all but a tiny fraction of the world's population, he just didn't care to brag about it.

Jimmie, 18 months younger, also served in the Navy during the war, deployed between the Philippines and Australia. The brothers had no communication for about three years, having been stationed thousands of miles apart, but that somehow seemed appropriate because their lives were a world apart in many ways. Jimmie simply wasn't nearly as fortunate in the aspects of the genetic lottery regarding talent and appearance.

Even Angelo's media colleagues, all male, made note of his handsome features. According to Bob Collins, *The Indianapolis Star's* leading sportswriter at the time, the joke within the local fraternity of reporters and broadcasters was that Angelo looked like a Greek god while Jimmie looked like a "goddam Greek." Whether an original line or not, it was applicable. Jimmie, however, would prove dominant in the luck department.

+-+

Living in his hometown, immersed in the sports world and enjoying a measure of celebrity status, Angelo logically would have had an active social life with both men and women. Whether he was loving the single life or simply being choosy, he didn't marry until he was 34 years old. On Jan. 4, 1954, he wed a local department store model, Joann Mings. Beneath a large photograph of the bride, the *News* noted she wore a "candlelight white silk cocktail suit with jeweled collar" and off-white accessories.

Their union was by all accounts as blissful as their wedding had been stylish. Not surprisingly, they were a glamour couple, popular in prominent social circles. The *News* once ran a photo of them in its society section, looking back over their shoulders while seated at a table during the Indianapolis Press Club's Front Page Ball at the Columbia Club.

Joann (also frequently spelled JoAnn in newspaper accounts) had her own knack for attracting attention. Tony Hinkle, Butler's longtime basketball coach, compared her beauty to that of silent film star Theda

Angelo poses with his wife, Joann, and friends Nancy and Danny Folsom following the Folsoms' wedding. It wasn't in his nature to clown. (Courtesy Danny Folsom)

Bara, an analogy fitting for a fiftyish man in the fifties. She made an impression in other ways, too, such as for her charming naivete. One of Angelo's closest friends, Danny Folsom, recalled being with Angelo and Joann at a banquet with baseball legend Stan Musial when Joann innocently asked Musial what he did for a living. Another time she met an executive from the Kimberly-Clark Corporation and exclaimed, "Oh, you make Kotex!"

Regardless, she never overshadowed Angelo, who was prominent beyond his newspaper byline. In a later era he likely would have expanded his career to broadcast media, but in the fifties his options were more limited. He was a popular featured attraction at public events, however. In 1953, for example, he spoke to high school students about sports writing at the annual Journalism Field Day, later spoke on the same topic to the Women's Press Club of Indiana and then was the principal speaker at Purdue's annual postseason football banquet in Lafayette. Those at least were the engagements that merited newspaper coverage; there likely were others.

He also played in a media basketball game pitting the city's newspaper staffers — called "Press" in that era — against a team of radio broadcasters before an Olympians NBA game that year. Although 34 years old at the time, he was his team's leading scorer — not much to brag about given the competition but another vehicle in which he reigned supreme in his profession.

Angelo was mostly popular for his personality and character, however.

George Theofanis, who would become Butler's head basketball coach from 1970-78, succeeding Hinkle, grew up near the Angelopolous family and shared their Greek heritage. Not long before he passed away in 2011, his memories of Angelo's influence were clear.

"He was one of the best guys I ever met in my life," Theofanis said. "In fact, I'm halfway crying right now as you're talking to me, because I loved him that much. He was like a brother to me. I had two brothers, but he was like another one."

Theofanis recalled an occasion when he climbed the stairs to visit Angelo at the family's home above the grocery store, looked inside, saw Angelo sitting at a table with his back turned and took the opportunity to sneak in and scare him.

"George, you don't do that," Angelo scolded gently. "You just don't do that."

"I'm sorry," Theofanis said.

"That's all right," Angelo said.

"He taught me the things I wasn't taught at home," Theofanis recalled.

Folsom, who met Angelo through his wife's friendship with Joann, had grown up in orphanages and foster homes. His mother died when he was three years old and his illiterate father was incapable of raising him, so he was farmed out. He built a successful business career as an adult but suffered another blow when he lost his five-year-old daughter to leukemia. He considered Angelo a mentor and confidant, the friend he could go to with his problems.

Nearly 50 years after Angelo's passing, Folsom also choked up while talking about him. "He was just the perfect guy," Folsom said. "He made an impression on everybody he ever met. He didn't have an enemy in the world."

Although Angelo was likely the city's most prominent media figure in an era when newspapers ruled that landscape, there's no evidence he inspired jealousy or resentment among his colleagues. Bob Doeppers, a photographer for the *News* and a fellow Navy veteran of World War II, always looked forward to sharing a ride to events with Angelo because he enjoyed his informative and humorous stories. He also appreciated Angelo's generosity while interacting with him at the Speedway in the May days leading up to the Indianapolis 500.

"He was a good egg," Doeppers said. "He always tried to do his best to help us, particularly at the Speedway. If a photographer was going out on his own for the day, if you could find him, he was a big help. Other guys on the staff didn't want to be bothered."

Another photographer, Joe Young, joined the *News* in 1958, when Angelo was no longer a full-time staff member but still covered some events. The routine when the newspaper's photographers and writers traveled together was for the photographer to drive. Theirs could have been an awkward pairing, the veteran celebrity writer and the newbie photographer, but Young recalls his trips with Angelo fondly.

"He was a gentleman," Young said. "He was such a pleasure to go with on assignments."

Doeppers' summary analysis could have served as a fitting epitaph for Angelo: "He never met anybody who forgot about meeting him." That, however, would have come off as too egotistical for Angelo's tastes.

Angelo was equally popular among the people he covered, particularly the coaches. Bill Sylvester, who progressed from star quarterback to football coach to athletic director at Butler, recalled Ohio State football coach Woody Hayes — who also served in the Navy in World War II — having extended conversations with Angelo. Folsom remembered Ohio State basketball coach Fred Taylor, who served in the Air Force in World War II, inviting Angelo into his team's locker room after a game at Butler. Folsom also said Angelo hit it off with Chicago Bears coach George Halas, a World War I veteran, at the Bears training camp.

Angelo enjoyed meeting sports celebrities and covering prestigious events, but his checked ego enabled him to cover everyday people and proceedings just as happily. He once headed over to the downtown YMCA on Senate Ave. — known locally as the "Colored Y" because it was the only one in Indianapolis that accepted African Americans — on a hot summer day to write about the pickup basketball games featuring some of the city's best players. He also covered amateur championships and youth league events in other sports.

He ventured out of the sports world, too. One of his best-remembered contributions to the *News* was the multi-part series he wrote on a solo trip to Greece, his father's homeland, and other European cities in 1951.

Two of the highlights of Angelo's newspaper career came within a 10-week window in 1955 — one article about a joyful triumph and the other of a horrifying tragedy.

He had championed the Attucks basketball program that sliced through social headwinds to become the first all-Black school in the country to win a state championship, and the first from Indianapolis to win in Indiana. The historical significance of that achievement was an elephant-in-the-room angle, but most of the state's sportswriters ignored it or tap-danced around it.

Angelo took dead aim, immediately acknowledging the transcendent aspects of the triumph. His column all at once displayed his talent, empathy, and humble nature. It began:

> You plant yourself in front of a typewriter and try to marshal thoughts and feelings. You know there is going to be a lot of staring at the keyboard in some vague hope that the letters will assemble themselves.
>
> The task of describing the reactions of the principals in the annual drama of the Indiana high school basketball tournament championship is difficult enough; when sociology is involved also in the drama you feel that a restricted talent is bound even tighter.

A Negro team, for the first time, has won the highest athletic honor the state has to covet ... and you want to say that man, at least in this little section of the world, has taken a step forward.

That article appeared in the March 21 edition of the *News*. His May 31 submission came from the opposite end of the sporting spectrum when Vukovich, winner of the 1953 and '54 "500s" and leader of the '55 race, was swept up in a backstretch accident and killed. Angelo and Vukovich were close friends despite Vukovich's resistance to letting people into his circle. So close, in fact, that Jimmie recalled Angelo once rushed over to the house where Vukovich and his wife stayed in May to retrieve the racing shoes Vukovich had forgotten the morning of the race.

Writing about such a tragedy would have been difficult no matter the victim, but Angelo that day had to recall the emotional strength formed by his war experience. He had been assigned to write the main story for the *News*, a full day's work on its own because the paper put out multiple editions as the race progressed. That story would have to be about Bob Sweikert's victory under the cloud cover of tragedy. Angelo, however, also wrote a column on Vukovich. It was an even-handed, professional tribute in which he acknowledged their friendship but served the interests of the readers ahead of his own.

Of Vukovich, he wrote:

> Under the crust and behind the calculated hyperbole he spread among fellow race drivers, there was a warm soul in this tremendous two-time 500-Mile Race winner hell-bent for a third straight triumph. He had a sense of humor, backed by a crinkly grin, that brought a smile even to those who had just taken the full force of his barb. He could peel the hide off the man who took himself too seriously, and Bill took himself seriously least of all.

Angelo praised Vukovich's integrity above all else, writing, "In this day and age of much duplicity and hypocrisy and 'conning,' Bill Vukovich came closest to being the completely honest man."

Angelo followed up the next day with coverage of the annual Victory Banquet, where prize winnings were distributed amid proceedings numbed by Vukovich's death. And then he took most of the summer off. He wrote a story on the city amateur tennis championship in July and another on a youth baseball clinic in August but nothing more in those months. He was supposed to join the annual September media tour of Big Ten schools and Notre Dame to gather information for football previews, but *News* sports editor Bill Fox reported Angelo had been admitted to Methodist Hospital because of "aches and pains."

He took all of September off from writing and wrote only sparingly in October before resuming a more normal pace of work in November.

It was never announced, but Angelo had been diagnosed with leukemia that year. Logic would indicate that was the primary reason for his sabbatical, although it wouldn't be surprising if mourning Vukovich was a factor as well. Angelo never wrote about his illness and mentioned it only to family and close friends, but over time the visual evidence of his physical decline became too painfully obvious to ignore.

Years later, Joann told me she received a letter from a government office informing her that nine of the 16 pilots in Angelopolous' Navy squadron had contracted the blood disorder because of the radiation absorbed from flights over Japan.

She also said she and Angelo went to the Mayo Clinic in Rochester, Minn. at some point. That might have been where his diagnosis was confirmed, or perhaps he sought treatment there. Whether that was before, after, or instead of his reported visit to Methodist Hospital is unknown.

The life-altering events of 1955 led Angelo to a life-altering decision. He left the *News* as a full-time staff member in 1956 to become a freelancer, a decision announced to the public in the paper's May 4 edition. He was kept on the payroll with a partial salary but was free to write for national magazines and other newspapers and — most of all — to work on the manuscript for this book. He and Joann moved to Ridgefield, New Jersey, 15 miles from Manhattan, to improve his access to major sporting events and her access to the New York City modeling world.

Angelo wrote magazine stories, including one on former Crispus Attucks High School star Oscar Robertson for *The Saturday Evening Post*, but still sent frequent articles to the *News*. Anyone with a Hoosier connection passing through the area was fair game for a story, whether it was an athlete or not. He wrote one on Indiana University President and United Nations delegate Herman B Wells, who spoke in Manhattan on Russia's Sputnik program.

Mostly, though, Angelo stuck to sports. He rhapsodized on Robertson, star of the Attucks state championship teams in 1955 and '56, at every opportunity, such as the article for the *News* that covered Robertson's 56-point game in Madison Square Garden during Robertson's sophomore season at the University of Cincinnati. Angelo met up with Robertson again a month later in Philadelphia when Robertson scored 43 points and grabbed 15 rebounds.

Angelo began that story:

> The saga of Oscar Robertson, basketball player, has reached the chapter where our young hero has discovered that wherever he goes away from home the joint is full of Missourians: They've got to be shown.

> The printed and spoken word about Oscar's magnificence has been shown so profusely throughout the land that Indiana's pride and joy (on loan to the University of Cincinnati) is reaping the inevitable harvest of doubt among those who haven't seen him. They reserve their right to scoff and come to exercise it.

He also was well-positioned in November of 1957 to capture the crushing disappointment of another prominent Indianapolis high school basketball player, former Attucks and Harlem Globetrotters standout Willie Gardner. The 6-foot-7 Gardner had played just a season-and-a-half at Attucks because of academic issues but was regarded as great a talent ever to come out of an Indiana high school. He went on to play a season for the Globetrotters, went into military service for two years, then added another season with the Globetrotters before the NBA New York Knicks drafted him.

Gardner had been voted the Globetrotters' Most Valuable Player each of his seasons with the team and owner Abe Saperstein called him "the greatest player I ever had." He also impressed his Knicks teammates and coaches in training camp. He quickly moved into the starting lineup and Knicks teammate Mel Hutchins was heard to declare, "We've got the answer to Bill Russell." It was quite a compliment, comparing the barely tested rookie to the blossoming NBA icon.

Gardner, however, was soon diagnosed with a heart murmur during a routine examination, and while he had experienced no discomfort, he eventually was diagnosed to have had a "silent heart attack" and was forced into retirement.

Angelo visited Gardner's Manhattan hotel room to write a first-hand account that read in part:

> "Through at 24. I can't believe it. I can't believe it." His voice trails off, he rubs his palms, he looks out the window, through only a narrow vent in the venetian blind he has permitted himself.

All in all, Angelo wrote 32 stories for the *News* in 1957, with datelines from New York, Philadelphia, New Jersey and Indianapolis. He wrote 34 stories for the paper in 1958, and also contributed text for Bob Verlin's photo book on the 500, "The Race." He wrote 57 *News* stories in 1959, 44 with New York datelines.

❖

His health in gradual but relentless decline, Angelo returned to Indianapolis with Joann in May of 1960 to help cover the "500." Joann broke an ankle in an auto accident on June 1, which was reported in the *News* sports section, but they received one bit of good news around that time when Angelo received word his article on race driver Jimmy Bryan for *True Magazine* had been selected for inclusion in the annual book *Best Sports Stories.* It was his third such honor.

Angelo and Joann returned to New Jersey in mid-June to resume their lives in the northeast but came back to Indianapolis for good in August. By then Angelo's doctors had given him no hope of recovery and he was becoming less independent.

The transition from New York correspondent to back-home-again-in-Indiana newsman was sudden. The *News* ran his story on baseball star Rocky Colavito, a former member of the Triple-A Indianapolis Indians, on Aug. 18, 1960, with a New York dateline. It must have been filed much earlier, though, because the next day they published his story on former heavyweight boxing champion Archie Moore speaking with inmates at the Indiana Reformatory in Pendleton.

Angelo soldiered on for the next two years from his home city. He wrote several stories for the entertainment section to avoid the physical strain of covering games, such as the Purdue Glee Club's fundraising performance at the Lebanon High School gymnasium in September. He later wrote a story off an interview with Dick Martin of the comedy team Rowan and Martin, who were appearing at a local nightclub.

Despite his stubborn optimism about a recovery, Angelo increasingly had to rely on the help of friends. Folsom drove him to some interviews, such as at the Bears' training camp at St. Joseph's College in Rensselaer, 100 miles north of Indianapolis. Other stories came to him. Some publicity-seeking actors and musicians performing in the city went to his residence to be interviewed.

His last sports story for the *News* appeared on Aug. 30, 1962. It was a tribute to the paper's retiring sports editor, Fox, who had hired him out of college. Angelo had just attended a dinner for Fox along with the rest of the sports staff. He had less than two months to live and the toll of his disease was painfully obvious in the group photograph that appeared in the paper.

"You knew he was dying," recalls Lyle Mannweiler, who had joined the staff as a copy boy that summer and is the only surviving staff member from that time.

Angelo, nearly skeletal, was smiling in the photo, providing further evidence of his graceful acceptance of fate's sucker punch.

Of Fox, Angelo wrote:

> It's all been said by now — Bill's regard for all sports and sports people, his gentleness, compassion, willingness to knock himself out, fairmindedness, modesty and of course, his large talent.
>
> If there is any way to wrap him up it might be to say that all his professional life William Francis Fox Jr. has been trapped by a monstrous integrity that has never released him.

Angelo never would have claimed it, but his friends would have insisted those words applied equally to himself.

If anyone ever deserved to write a farewell column, a common indulgence for retiring sportswriters, Angelo did. After all, his own story was more dramatic than those of most of the people he wrote about. But his last article, appearing on Sept. 3, was a soft feature on a local couple, Charles and Pearl Enders, both of whom worked for the downtown Block's department store. Charles was a suit salesman of Greek heritage. Pearl was a model of German heritage. Perhaps the then-unusual crossover of their nationalities caught Angelo's eye. Or, perhaps, one or both of the Enders were friends of Joann, and he wrote it as a favor to her.

Angelo died on Oct. 14, 1962, after being bed-ridden for a few weeks in the apartment he and Joann rented. He was 43 years old. Looking at it one way, his life was cruelly cut short. Another way, he was a war fatality who got to live another 17 years before his exposure to the radiation in Japan finally captured him.

His fame and reputation were such that brief wire service obituaries ran in newspapers throughout the United States and in Canada — from Carlsbad, New Mexico to Jersey City, New Jersey to Sapulpa, Oklahoma, to San Francisco and even into Windsor, Ontario. The response in Indiana, meanwhile, was personal and passionate. He wasn't just a journalist, he was an admired sports figure throughout the state.

The Journal and Courier in Lafayette called him "one of every sportswriter's favorite guys," adding "he never wrote anything ugly because it was impossible for him to think that way. Angie knew how to write and how to live."

A sportswriter for *The Noblesville Ledger* told of a favor Angelo had done for his sister. She and her family were moving out of their apartment in Indianapolis, below the one in which Angelo spent his final days. While the family loaded their belongings, he volunteered to sit in their living room to guard against theft.

"I'm sorry I can't help you, but I can at least watch for you," he told them.

The *News* published an article on Angelo's passing on Page 1 of the second section rather than in the sports pages, as well as a tribute on the editorial page. It followed a day later with another story and a four-photo spread of him from various points in his newspaper career.

The rival *Star*, meanwhile, treated Angelo like one of its own, running an extensive obituary and editorial. It also published the best of all the tributes to Angelo, from Bob Collins.

> When a newspaperman dies, his comrades usually give him a stature in eulogies that he perhaps never enjoyed in life.
>
> Thus the most obscure copy reader becomes, from the typewriter of a grieving friend, a sort of latter day giant of journalism who, daily, had the world at his fingertips.
>
> It is a failing; albeit a compassionate failing for which we surely can be forgiven.
>
> So I am writing this just in case anybody thinks that may be the way it is with the things they are writing and saying about Angelo. All the good things they say about him are true.
>
> Angelo was class — all the way.
>
> Few people wore as well on their fellow men as did Angelo Angelopolous. He was the embodiment of an old lost belief that you do not have to shout to be heard, nor push to reach the front. Angie made it all the way to the top without leaving his footprint on a single neck.

XX ● VUKOVICH: THE MAN WHO WOULDN'T LIFT

English, used properly, is a beautiful language. And Angie was master of all its subtleties. He could turn a phrase, this man could, and he had a feel for people and a rare ability to transmit emotion — and belief — to paper.

I remember first reading his stuff years ago, and thinking, "If there are many in this business as good as him, I'll starve to death." And I remember my joyful surprise upon later discovering that he was the warmest and kindest of men, a delightful companion, a friend who would back you to the limit — and fierce competition.

You want to know the kind of person he was? It was like this: if your wife or girlfriend remarked that he was one of the handsomest men she'd ever seen you weren't irritated. You were proud she had brains enough to recognize it.

Just seven years ago he had the world by the handle. He was young, talented and recognized as one of the greatest newspaper writers ever produced in this city. He was gaining a national reputation. It was just a matter of time, we all said, until he left us.

Then it hit, that horrible word: Leukemia.

You measure a man by the way he meets adversity. I never knew a man who tried as hard to continue a normal life under such a burden. And all the time he fought it; with every sinew of muscle, with every ounce of will. Not once, until the final days, did he swerve from the belief that he would win.

Even down near the end when there was nothing left of this splendid, handsome man but a wasted body and the sight of him was like a knife in the stomach of his friends, he would say, "I think I am making progress."

Only when he had nothing left to fight with did he die. And his friends will continue to say what they have been saying for seven years, not in pity, but with sincerity and pride that, "there was a man."

So you read all the things they will write and say about Angelo. And you can believe every word of it.

Angelo was class — all the way.

✦

Bob Dietz once told me Angelo, in his final days, extracted the promise of a favor from *News* management: make sure Jimmie stays employed. Jimmie had been active in journalism in high school and college and landed a job after the war with *The Indianapolis Times.* The *Times,* however, was the city's third-in-circulation newspaper and by the early sixties was struggling to survive. Lacking Angelo's gift for arranging words, Jimmie's future was hardly secure.

The promise was kept. The *Times'* final issue was published on Oct. 11, 1965. Jimmie's first story in the *News* appeared on Oct. 22 and he remained there until retiring in 1991. His assignments took him to 67 countries and six Olympic Games, and he was inducted into five halls of fame.

Jimmie remained single and lived with two of his three sisters throughout his adult life before dying in 2009, age 88. He often was the butt of jokes for his odd appearance and quirky personality but was impossible to dislike because of his positive spirit and decency. He remained an ardent admirer of his older brother to the very end.

"He was a brain, I'll tell you that," Jimmie told me a few months before passing. "He never gave me any, though. I kept asking him for it. He said, 'Get your own damn brain.' He was about a hundred years smarter than me."

Joann threw her wedding ring into Angelo's grave as his casket was lowered in the Greek section of Crown Hill Cemetery and never remarried. Folsom joked years later that Angelo was so tight with his money that he would have "jumped out of the box" to salvage it if he could have. Joann stayed busy in the fashion world following her modeling career. She took a job in 1968 as a fashion designer and buyer for Davidson's, a women's clothing store in Indianapolis, and her name recognition was sufficient that when she opened her own store in Greenwood in the late Seventies, she called it Joann Angelopolous Dress Apparel.

Joann moved into a senior care facility in her later years, before it was necessary according to friends, but assisted the workers there in

Butler coach Tony Hinkle presents Joann Angelopolous a citation from President John F. Kennedy before the January 16, 1963 game against Ball State that raised funds for a leukemia fund in Angelo's name.
(Photo by Joe Young)

various activities and served on the Governor's Task Force for the Aged. She died of cancer on Dec. 28, 2014, age 83. She donated her body to the Indiana University Medical School, so no formal funeral service or burial was conducted.

Friends wishing to honor her were asked to donate to the Angelo Angelopolous Scholarship Fund for journalism students at Butler, an award established in 1993. The fund still exists, one of many ways Angelo's name has been kept alive over the years.

Butler also formed a leukemia fund in Angelo's name, which it announced in January of 1963. A photograph in the *News* showed Tony Hinkle — who had been an honorary pallbearer at Angelo's funeral — presenting a citation from President John F. Kennedy to Joann the day before Butler's Jan. 16 game with Ball State. Butler's dance team, the "Halftime Honeys," walked through the crowd of 8,225 fans at halftime and extracted $1,147.25 in bills and loose change for the fund. More donations were raised by other means on campus, such as a "faculty auction" during Greek Week in which students bid for the services of faculty members for one day.

The university also posthumously awarded Angelo its highest honor, the Butler Medal, in June of 1963. It is still given annually to an alumnus for career achievement and community service.

The *News*, meanwhile, established the Angelo Angelopolous Memorial Fund for leukemia research immediately following his death. Administration of the fund was handled by a committee of Indianapolis sportswriters and broadcasters, all said to be close friends with Angelo.

Mailed donations were accepted and the Indianapolis Warriors semi-pro football team's game on Oct. 28 was declared a benefit game, with half of the proceeds from the sale of $2 tickets turned over to the fund. It raised more than $1,300.

It is unknown how long the two leukemia funds survived. Both are believed to have been turned over to the Indianapolis Chapter of the Leukemia Society, Inc. The disease, however, remains as great a threat today as ever.

The American Auto Racing Writers and Broadcasters Association also moved to honor Angelo, by initiating a sportsmanship award in his name in 1963. It was presented annually through 2015 and sporadically since then.

Perhaps the most unique indication of Angelo's popularity was that an Indianapolis high school, Arlington, named the mental attitude award given to a senior athlete in his honor. Angelo had no connection with the school, which opened in 1961, but Arlington's athletic director, Charlie Maas, was a 1949 Butler graduate and, like many who passed through the university, a friend of Angelo's. He likely initiated the honor. It was first presented in 1963 to three-sport athlete Steve Loman, who went on to become an optometrist. Loman was an appropriate inaugural winner. He possessed many of Angelo's positive traits but also faced some of life's cruelest equalizers in his later years, including dementia and Parkinson's disease. The award was presented to Arlington senior athletes at least through 1971. The school became a junior high in 2018.

The Angelo Angelopolous Sportsmanship Award was first presented to Arlington High School senior Steve Loman in 1963.

Angelo's name lived on most frequently in memories, however. Folsom said whenever he traveled to sporting events in other states, such as the Masters

Angelo's illness had aged him prematurely, but he neither complained about it nor hid from it.

golf tournament in Georgia, and mentioned he was from Indianapolis, people routinely asked if he knew Angelo Angelopolous. Tom Keating, a general columnist for the *Star*, attended the National Baseball Hall of Fame's induction ceremony in Cooperstown, N.Y. in 1977, when legendary sports columnist Red Smith was honored. Upon meeting Keating and learning he was from Indianapolis, Smith immediately asked if he knew Angelo.

"He was such a class guy, one of the most charming people I've ever met," Smith told Keating.

❧❧

This book, then, reunites two beloved friends whose lives and careers fatefully merged and then were tragically cut short. Bill Vukovich, without question, was the greatest race driver of his era. Judging a sportswriter is far more subjective, but Angelo Angelopolous was established as one of the greatest of his profession. Both excelled but left behind unfinished business.

Converting Angelo's manuscript into this book turned out to be more challenging and time-consuming than I first envisioned (isn't it always?) but hopefully it stands as an accurate reflection of both men. I tried to edit Angelo's words in a manner that maintains his graceful style while also accounting for the fact more than 60 years have passed since he wrote them. Mrs. Lawrence Thompson, for example, now goes by her first name, Dorcas. And Vukovich's profanity, which had been crossed out by hand, has been restored. Surely readers won't be shocked to learn race drivers from that era occasionally uttered words in private conversation not suited for Sunday School.

Angelo made one of his final public appearances when members of The Indianapolis News *sports staff gathered to honor retiring editor Bill Fox. Leukemia had nearly finished him off by this point; he passed away six weeks later. Front row, from left: Ray Marquette, Wayne Fuson, Bill Fox, Les Koelling, Angelo. Back row: J.E. O'Brien, Frank Wilson, Corky Lamm, Bob Renner, Lyle Mannweiler.* (Courtesy Joe Young)

Angelo's tombstone at Crown Hill Cemetery is appropriate for a humble, uncomplicated man. (Photo by Mark Montieth)

I also changed Angelo's vague self-references to first person. He mentions "the newsman" or "a sportswriter" in scenes in which he appeared. Perhaps he was being modest, his nature, but it seemed awkward and unnecessary. Angelopolous and Vukovich were close friends, which was more acceptable in that era of journalism than today, and this book benefits from that relationship in that private conversations are included that no other journalist could have known about. There's no sense hiding it.

I made only one factual change. Angelo wrote simply that Vukovich's father died. The truth is that John Vukovich took his own life, a well-known detail among Vukovich family members and their friends. Billy Vukovich Jr. mentioned it often in his later years, I'm told.

I also rearranged some chapters. Angelo alternated lead-ins to the 1955 race with flashbacks to previous races but I thought a chronological build-up after the opening chapter would be easier to follow. I didn't want to edit a supreme writer's work with a heavy hand, but the manuscript clearly was unfinished and in need of some rescue.

Angelo titled his book, "The Man Who Wouldn't Lift" because of Vukovich's bold driving style. Cars in that era reached 180 mph on the straights but didn't have the aerodynamics to maintain that speed in the turns. Vukovich won because he kept his foot on the throttle longer than other drivers. He was strong enough and brave enough to wrestle his car through the turns while others were letting up.

Angelo didn't lift, either. He wrote for as long as his withering body permitted, returning to his typewriter until he simply couldn't go on. Despite all the tributes, memorials, and memories he inspired, his primary legacy should be his written words. Hopefully this collection of them, tardy as it is, will stand as his greatest triumph.

VUKOVICH

The Man Who Wouldn't Lift

The Speedway home of Lawrence and Dorcas Thompson, where Bill and Esther stayed during the month of May. It was an easy walk from here to the main gate at the track. (Photo by Mark Montieth)

1

"You know, I think I'm going to need it."

Man in a Hurry

On the morning of the race Bill awoke late. He shaved and dressed, hurriedly, then kissed Esther. A few minutes later he kissed her again. Esther, a little puzzled, asked, "What was that for?"

Bill grinned. "Can't a man kiss his own wife?"

When he was ready to leave the house, just before 7, he pulled out his wallet. He took out a dollar bill and gave the remainder of the money, wallet and all, to Esther. She tried to hand it back, puzzled. But Bill insisted. "I won't be needing it. All I need is this dollar for breakfast."

As he made for the door Dorcas Thompson, with whom Bill and Esther stayed during the month of May, called after him: "Good luck, Bill!" He stopped and replied: "Thanks. You know, I think I'm going to need it."

Bill Vukovich had never done any of those things on the day of the Indianapolis 500 — rising late, doubling back to kiss his wife a second time, surrendering his wallet and other personal belongings, pausing to reply to Dorcas' yearly sendoff. He usually only waved at Dorcas, or perhaps yelled, "Thanks" on the run. His reference to luck was the most unusual thing, though. He acknowledged that element of racing but had never alluded to it on a race day. At least he didn't stop to talk about it.

This gave Dorcas even more pause at the end of a month she felt was out of kilter. Even when Esther had asked her if she wanted tickets for the race, an almost perfunctory ritual she and Esther performed annually, she had hesitated to accept. But, unable to understand her own uncertainty, she finally responded, slowly: "Yes … Yes, I'll go."

Bill left the house through the front door and began walking down Fifteenth Street. In other years he had cut through the Thompsons' backyard to avoid the swelling crowds for as long as possible, but there was no escaping them for long. Sixteenth Street, the primary artery to the Speedway, was flooded with fans swerving their way around automobiles that creeped bumper to bumper for miles in unbroken chains from all directions. The pedestrians were moving faster despite the burden of picnic equipment, the metal drink coolers and sandwich baskets.

On this race day they were weighed down further by jackets and rain apparel, for this was not the normal Memorial Day in Indianapolis. The temperature was in the mid-50s, well below the norm. Two years earlier, it had even reached the 90s. When the gates opened at 5 a.m. there was the usual frenzied motorized land rush for the prime infield positions along the inside fences, but this time engines were kept running to enable the use of the car heaters.

Regardless, 175,000 fans were streaming into the Indianapolis Motor Speedway from every state of a speed-conscious country. They came also from the other Americas and from Europe. And in some years, from Asia. The first fan, a weather-creased, railroad-capped man named Larry Bisceglia, always arrived seven weeks before the race to begin his wait outside the track, and hundreds of automobiles are lined up at the eleven gates with three days still to go. By midnight on race morning, 2,500 cars were in line.

Vukovich was making his way to this spectacle in his rapid stride, head down, glancing only briefly at the glutted streets. Speedway City now held a temporary population of 50,000 transients. Some had stubbornly managed a few winks of sleep during the night on makeshift pallets in cars or trucks, but most had simply wandered about, hoping to be entertained by others no more entertaining than themselves. Intermittent light drizzle harassed them. Impromptu refreshment stands operated on the main roads, their strong odors filling the air. The follow-the-crowd food merchants were getting competition from one gate-side resident who offered a breakfast of eggs, bacon, toast and coffee for $1.

Checkered flags … checkered hats … souvenir pillows … tickets scalped at $4 above face value … souvenir photos in a beat-up race car … a look at a two-headed calf … a ride on a carousel or a Ferris wheel. Hawkers, pitchmen, promoters … weight-guessing, ring-tossing … hot dogs, pizza, caramel corn … evangelists competing against game-of-chance hucksters … service stations selling use of their restrooms, from 10 cents to a quarter. All through the night.

The cold and rain had combined to make the throng unusually orderly. When the 5 a.m. gate-opening bomb went off, 10,000 automobiles had lurched forward, engines defining the dawn. The first to roll had set up a clinking, clanging racket as they crunched over beer cans, bottles, trash, debris. Many farther back in the lines were impatient; they leaned on their horns. Traffic was sometimes three abreast, sometimes four, sometimes even six.

Policemen — 400 of them — and track guards shouted directions. In fifty-one minutes, the incredible jam at the gates had dissipated, as those fans without reserved seats raced each other to infield vantage points. Most relied on their height to be able to witness the action on the track but others, more mechanically minded, erected towers and lifts, some going thirty feet into the air.

Some stretched out and tried to get a bit more sleep. Some of the boys started looking for girls; some of the girls hoped to be found. There were still several hours to go before 11 a.m., when the voice over the public address system would say, "Gentlemen, start your engines."

Now the traffic outside the track had settled down, moving steadily, a police airplane hovering overhead, dispersing the bottlenecks by ground-to-air phone. The 100,000 who had slept in their own beds or who had traveled part of the night were without anxiety, for they held tickets for seats.

This was the crowd Bill Vukovich fell in with as he walked toward the track. The wind whipped his jacket, and he was still fumbling with the zipper as he reached Speedway's Main Street. He spotted a rotund writer acquaintance, Jim Smith of *The Indianapolis Times*, with whom I was walking, and yelled, "Wait a minute, Fat Boy! I'll walk over with you if I can get this damn jacket buttoned."

Jim and I chided Bill about being late. "What's the hurry?" he shot back. "The race doesn't start until 11 o'clock. All I have to do is drive it, not push it." He stuffed his hands into his pockets and walked so swiftly we had to strain to keep up.

We walked north up Main Street toward the Speedway's main gate, Bill talking almost jauntily of the garage preparations. "Some guys spent all night plugging up firewalls for the cold. We didn't do a damned thing. It'll get warmer, wait and see." He stopped for an instant to comment on the scene around him: "Boy, what a carnival!"

He delayed but a few seconds, for he was only interested in getting to his garage as quickly as possible. Crowds made him uncomfortable. He liked people, but he disliked being accosted. He often said, "Love those paying customers," and he meant it. He believed a driver should give the fans his very best. But face to face he was shy with them. He had nothing to say and wanted to get away.

As we walked, we could hear murmurs in the crowd. "There's Vukovich." "There goes Vuky." He waved whenever someone called out to him. At the gate, three young boys asked for his autograph. He slowed down, and as he signed, he asked each his name, interested.

Credentials presented, we walked behind the grandstand and paddock, turned right, and walked across the track. Another right turn, behind the ancient Pagoda, and we were headed toward the garages.

The flags of the Ambassadors from South American countries who were in attendance this day snapped in the breeze behind the pit parquets, a festive touch. Bill didn't notice them. He wanted to get free from the crowd, have breakfast, and escape to the quiet of the garage so he could think about the race.

At the entrance to the garages, he said, "Well, I'll see you later."

He still couldn't escape the masses, however. Inside the fences surrounding Gasoline Alley were the friends of friends of drivers, mechanics and car owners — the pit workers, the stooges, the lap-prize donors, the accessory people, the press, radio, television and newsreel crowds. Many wished him luck. He nodded but avoided conversation.

He headed for the restaurant and hurried through breakfast. Then he called Esther, something he had never done from the track the day of a race.

"When are you coming?" he asked.

"We're coming," she said.

She returned the phone to the cradle, once again puzzled by his unusual display of emotion.

"I want to drive that thing."

Breeding Ground

A young man of 16 hunts for a yielding place in the fence. Beyond the barricade an auto race is taking place. The pitch of the shrieking engines is a siren call to the lad. This is Fresno, California, the biggest oasis in the San Joaquin Valley, where the temperature can climb to 110 degrees, an area where a lad, if he has the will, can rise above the horizon and make a mark. He can stand there and be honed by sun and heat and dust and occasional wind — or he can wilt.

Sometimes, as if nature wasn't severe enough, fate also helps shape the young man's spirit. This is Billy Vukovich, and hunting along the backstretch fence he is about to turn a corner in his life.

His father, John Vukovich, was a carpenter mill hand in Alameda, Calif., but his health was poor with the fog and dampness there. It was not like the sunny farm life of his native Yugoslavia. Soon after Billy's birth, the fifth of eight children and the youngest of three boys, his parents turned toward the warmer inland and settled in farm country, at small, hot, dusty Kerman, a wide bend twenty-two miles from Fresno. Now their breed would have room to grow on their forty acres and perhaps John and his wife, Mildred, could get back some of the feel of the Old Country.

Life was hard working the farm, but the family had the necessities. They tilled the soil, grew grapes and figs, milked the cows, made soap, and baked bread. The Vukoviches stayed in front, but just barely. Once, little Billy had to be hired out to a cotton grower to earn extra money for the family.

The eight children of John and Mildred Vucurovich. Front: Bill (age 23), Eli and Mike. Back: Ann, Florence, Dorothy, Mary and Jennie. (Courtesy Bob Gates)

Mama Vukovich was relieved merely to get the eight children into bed each night and so there was too little time for affections. Billy was content to be by himself, anyway. He grew silently. He didn't always reply when spoken to, but on occasion he'd express his feelings in a way that left little doubt what he was thinking. Mama always said, "He makes so much noise because he's so silent around the house."

By turns there was in the family a bicycle and a Shetland pony and even a Model T Ford. This was the grace in their lives. For the boys, Mike, Eli, and Billy, the Model T was a fascinating escape. One day the three took the car without permission. They were gone a long while and returned only in time for supper. Their father said nothing, supper was eaten and soon the three went to bed, with the disobedience yet to be broached. When the three were in bed, Papa Vukovich hunted up his green switch. Walking into the bedroom he whaled into three bottoms.

At times it seemed as if the three boys — Billy especially, whom Mama called "Vaso," in her native Slovenian — were born to speed. First there was the buggy, pulled by a pony. When the boys went to school, they urged the animal so fast around corners they were on only two of the four wheels. Papa check-matedly built a two-wheeler for them but Billy would ride even the cow when he could get away with it.

Then came the bike. When Billy was 7 and Mike 13, they would pedal the twenty-two miles from Kerman to Fresno's board track to watch the races. They would make the trip — Mike usually pedaling and trailing Billy on the back of his bike — a few days in advance to hunt out a tree they could climb, from where they could watch for free.

They even plowed with the tractor at full throttle, their centrifugal force so great they could only turn inside five rows instead of the normal three, but at that rate they could till a twenty-acre field in half a day, a job that normally required eight to ten hours. Then they'd hop off the speeding tractor and let it topple to a stop.

The Model T Ford was the greatest stimulus. When the parents left the house on Sundays to go into town, out came the car to be driven in breakneck fashion. It was overturned so often the boys decided to keep the top down permanently so that its battered state wouldn't betray them. Then they would hurriedly take to rakes to obliterate tell-tale ground marks. Once Billy overturned the car, stuck out his hand ("I was trying to hold it up," he later explained) and sprained a wrist and thumb. His mother caught him behind the house trying to soothe the injury with water. He wasn't yet in his teens.

Somehow Papa saved enough to make a down payment on a twenty-acre muscat grape and raisin vineyard, which they found a few miles down the road at Sanger. They carried their belongings with them down the highway.

Still keeping to himself when he had free time, Billy, in patched-up, handed-down overalls, would wander off into the high hedges of the vineyard and stay lost until someone came in search of him. Often in those times he would stare for hours at pictures of race cars and race drivers.

Two years after buying the vineyard, in 1932, the pressures became too much for John Vukovich. He took his own life, shooting himself. Little was said about it, then or forever, but it became part of the family lore. Billy was 14, Eli 15. They were the only boys now living at home and there was an ailing mother and farm to care for. They left school and took jobs picking grapes, chopping cotton, tilling fields, making 35 cents an hour. They drove trucks. Mike (who was always "Mick" to

Billy) joined in and they shot jackrabbits and coyotes, the latter for a bounty of $2.50 a hide. They speared salmon with a make-shift spear from a pitchfork. These were the days of the Great Depression, and the Vukoviches were living as if they were featured characters in John Steinbeck's novel, "The Grapes of Wrath."

The San Joaquin Valley experienced some of its worst frosts in history in those years. The Vukoviches (it had been "Vucurovich" until a naturalization judge suggested the easier spelling) held on for two years, but at the end of the second cold season the owner forced them to give back his frozen vineyard. They owed only $200 more but their pleas for another six months grace — until July — fell on deaf ears.

They rented another vineyard, but another frost and a bad raisin crop drove them off their beloved land and into Fresno to work for wages, when they could find jobs.

Fate had now colluded with nature to shape and mold Billy Vukovich. Already taciturn, he became even more introspective and determined.

※

On this day, Bill Vukovich, 16, was looking for a way to get into the Fresno Fairgrounds to watch an automobile race from the only seat he could afford: a free one on the fence. He found it — and found the driving force of his life. He already knew he wanted to race. Was it escape? Was it merely the thrill? Did he see in it the chance to confront a fate that had given him a hard row in life, had deprived him of a parent, and had ended his boyhood by the time he was 14?

Bill broke into midget racing at 16. He once took his mother to watch him race, but while she sat alone in the stands her "Vaso" crashed and went upside down. He was injured but the anguished Mama Vukovich still didn't speak English and couldn't make anyone understand her pleas. She had no one to turn to, could not get to him. Bill, in pain, could not reach her, either, but the more grievous hurt was the thought of her sitting alone and helpless. The image went deep within him and stayed. He never took her to another race. Four years later, Mildred Vukovich was gone, too.

At 17, Vukovich visited a hay barn ten miles from Fresno. A friend, Fred Gerhardt, owned and kept there a Chevrolet "roadster." Gerhardt was working on it in the light from the two open barn ends when Bill, wearing a T-shirt and blue jeans, quietly presented himself, silhouetted by the hot Valley sun.

"I want to drive that thing," he said.

Gerhardt didn't even look up.

Bill didn't budge.

"I want to drive that thing," he repeated.

Gerhardt turned his head from the engine.

"You want to kill yourself, boy?"

Bill left without answering. But he was back the next day and the next day and the next, repeating his desire. Gerhardt, feeling the force of the kid's determination, finally gave in.

In his first race, in choking dust, Bill won $25 for third place. The third race, he won. For the next few months, he drove the Chevy on all sorts of tracks. Gerhardt grew to love him and let him keep all the money he won. It wasn't much, $10-$15 for a good race, but someone finally had responded to this silent, determined young man.

Fresno's dusty Airport Speedway soon became Bill's playground. He competed in his first main event six weeks after his debut. A high school buddy, Fred DeOrian, was in the lead. On him, Bill started the treatment for which he would become famous — nerve warfare.

DeOrian, riding comfortably in the groove, looked back to see who was chasing him. There was Vukovich. They went into a turn. When they came out Bill's right front wheel was in front of DeOrian's left rear and only a foot out. Every time DeOrian glanced over, Bill's wheel would drift in front of Fred's. Nothing can cause two race cars to flip easier, should there be contact. A small mistake, and DeOrian would connect with Bill's wheel and he likely would be upside down.

Vukovich was matching nerve endings. He won.

Within a year Bill had graduated to midgets. In his first race he locked wheels with another car, flipped end over end, broke three ribs and a collarbone. Seven weeks later he was racing again.

That same year brother Eli started driving midgets, and in his first competition found himself facing his kid brother. Bill established the track relationship quickly. "Don't block me if there's pressure on," he said flatly. "Out on that track you're just another driver to me." Bill won that race, too. He seemed to race even harder against Eli, giving him no more quarter than anyone else.

Bill traveled like a gypsy, usually with Mike and Eli, trying to make fifteen to twenty races a week. He ate pork and beans out of a can and slept in the trailer that hauled the midget.

In a main event in Bakersfield, Bill got rough with Walt Faulkner, trying to bump him into the infield. Faulkner tired of the game and grew angry. He waited until Bill was coming out of a turn and all his weight was on the outside. Walt let him have it. Bill flipped three times before he flew through the fence. Faulkner got airborne also and ended up sliding along upside down.

When the dust cleared Faulkner was pulled out of his wreck. He looked around. Standing in front of him was Vukovich, pulling grass from his mouth, but like Faulkner, no more than scratched. Faulkner backed off, ready for a fight. Bill looked at him, then started grinning. "You know, Walt," he said, "you're not a bad guy at all."

Bill Vukovich could take it as well as give it. He and Walt became fast friends.

In another race he knocked Jimmy Bryan out of the groove. Bryan became so angered he retaliated and both drivers spun out of the race. Bill later approached Bryan and said, "You're all right. You're gonna be a race driver. There are only two of them now, me and (Troy) Ruttman."

And yet when he won, he never talked of his victory.

Eventually he wanted his own midget racer. Gerhardt had a Drake, but he wanted $750 for it and told Bill he didn't think he could save that much money. Thoroughly angered, Bill stalked off. Couldn't?

He became obsessed. A year later he walked into Gerhardt's garage and counted out $750. Gerhardt balked, but soon gave in. Bill had kept his part of the bargain.

The Drake became his "jewel." No mechanic ever loved or cared for a car more. He welded and welded and took apart and examined and

Vukovich earned his racing stripes in the midget and sprint car races in California in the 1940s, for little money and no glamour. (Ted Knorr collection)

threw away and replaced. And he patted the hood and told Esther, "I'm going to blow those chauffeurs off the track." On those evenings when he didn't win, he wouldn't sleep. There would be lights on through the night in his workshop and if a passerby peeked through the cracks of the shed, he would have seen Vukovich standing amid a gutted midget race car, trying to find an answer.

It seemed he was upside-down half the time. He raced as if on a bicycle, always on two wheels. He'd tinker with ways to improve speed at the expense of stability until he'd topple on his head again. Then he would tinker some more. Bruises, bumps, spins weren't important. The important thing was to win. He scarred his hands, broke his shoulders, smashed his ribs. At one track he went through the fence three times, at the same spot, all three times upside down. He walked away the third time and exclaimed, "I'm going to quit racing; it's costing too damned much for crash helmets."

Blow off the other chauffeurs he did. He often was called "The Mad Russian," a geographically inaccurate tag for a Serb, but progressively became known as "Win or Spin Vukovich." Some of the fans he met couldn't understand him. He frightened some, and some even hated him.

At Bayshore there was the business of the match race with the rival association's champ to determine the "hot dog" of the West Coast. Jerry Piper, racing on home grounds and starting on the outside, cut Bill off in the first turn. (He said later he'd figured that if Bill had been on the outside, he would have done the same thing.) Bill, who'd endured similar blocking treatment from Piper a week before at Fresno, was infuriated. He cut across the infield, rammed into Piper, and both went into the fence. Livid fans threw programs and seat cushions and paper onto the track to express their hatred of Bill Vukovich, and some came out of the stands and spit on his car. Bill couldn't understand why. Police hurried to restore peace and they escorted Bill and Esther away. Afterwards, Vukovich and Piper, while an angry crowd still milled around mob-like, enjoyed a mutual laugh at the incident. And Esther could joke, "It isn't everybody who gets a police escort."

There was something about the furious, uncompromising manner Bill went about winning that made even his bruised and battered conquests like him, even if spectators were appalled by their perceived ruthlessness and were frightened by the enormity of the risks he took.

Once at Los Angeles in a race with Troy Ruttman he drove so fiercely that aghast fans stood and yelled, "Stop! Stop! Stop!" And when Bill pulled into the pits, not understanding, he asked innocently what all the yelling was about.

One night Bill was running third and his good friend, Earl Motter, second. Once again unwilling to fit into the single file of cars that inevitably occurred in some midget races because there was but one best, narrow path, Bill cut through the infield and bumped the leader out, flipping him. The collision dropped him back, so he cut through the infield again and rammed his buddy Motter, turning him over, too. Bill won the race. Or, rather, he finished first. The judges took the victory away, granting him only third place.

He apologized to Earl, saying, "I had no brakes." Earl gave him a short, "Yeh, yeh." Bill insisted, "Come and see them." But Earl, pointing to his identical set of brakes, replied, without moving, "That's all right; here are your brakes."

In a later race Earl decided to take Bill's advice and nudge people out of the way to gain position. The first time he tried it he flipped over. He crawled out of the midget to find Vukovich doubled up with laughter. Earl resolved, as he said later with a smile, "not to take the man's advice anymore."

An in-race feud between Vukovich and Al Heath set West Coast fans astir for months. Heath had boasted he would run Vukovich into the Gilmore Stadium grandstand for shutting the gate on him — the hazardous but effective move of cutting across the track to block a competitor and prevent him from passing. For thirty laps Bill shut the gate on Heath. Then Heath outwitted him. He faked an attempt to pass high on the outside. When Bill slid over to block him, Heath jammed his throttle to the floorboard and screamed past Bill on the inside.

Twenty-thousand fans were then chilled by a frightening sight. Vukovich, at a mile-a-minute speed, began bumping the rear of Heath's car. With the threat of a major accident, race officials frantically waved "stop" flags — until Heath gave up. He turned wide and Bill sped past him to victory.

Eli, meanwhile, remained just another driver. Bill had warned his brother about trying a maneuver Eli had in mind. Bill said it wouldn't work. Eli tried it and narrowly avoided disaster. Afterwards, Bill wouldn't go over to where Eli had crashed to check on him. When someone assured him Eli was all right, Bill spat: "Serves him right!"

Was he a man so bent on winning he could think of nothing else? So determined to be first that everyone else, while on the track, was an enemy, even his brother? Or a man so dedicated to a goal that he couldn't compromise? Or a man with a soft center who built a hard crust because he was afraid that if he let his guard down it would be pierced — and he would be undone? He surely remembered the times Mike and Eli had rushed to pull him out of his car after he had turned upside down.

There was a race in Gilmore Stadium in Los Angeles. A rich main event, a 100-lapper, for $1,200. His good friend, Faulkner, had said, "I'm going to win that go." Bill had replied, "The hell you are." And they warned each other to stay the hell out of the way.

There were thirteen other drivers, but it became a duel between Vukovich and Faulkner. Walt took the lead and held it. Try as hard as he could, Bill couldn't get by. He probed underneath in the turns. He tried to bluff. He pushed Faulkner's car from behind. He seemed to be in Walt's cockpit half the time. Nothing doing. Faulkner had been around, too. The fortieth lap came. Bill was exasperated. He started to play rougher. Hugging the inside rail, he wedged himself between it and Faulkner, got under him, actually nudged Walt sideways, and took him up across the track and into the outside fence — and then straightened and went on to win the race. Faulkner was fortunate to finish second. Esther was sitting with Mary Faulkner. Glumly, she figured Bill was in one of his moods.

Bill received the checkered flag to a chorus of boos from another angry crowd. A friend scolded him. "That's the dirtiest driving I ever saw." Bill was belligerent. "What are you going to do about it!" American Automobile Association officials who were supervising the event were up in arms. They wanted to suspend Bill, but Walt barked back at them: "Listen, dammit; this is between me and Vukovich. It's no one else's damn business."

Neither Bill nor Esther said a word as they left the track and headed for Fresno. Once on the road, however, she began to lecture him. "You shouldn't have done that," she said quietly, and continued more severely. Bill still said not a word.

When they arrived home Bill called the promoter. He told him to give Walt first-place money and him second. The reply: "No, Bill. Walt says it's all right. You'll get first and Walt second."

Faulkner, meanwhile, had gone home to Long Beach. The next morning his phone rang.

"Hey, Faulkner." It was Vukovich, calling from Fresno.

"Yeh."

"Hey, Faulkner!"

"What the hell do you want?" Walt recognized the voice.

"I'm sending the check over."

"Nuts to you. I don't want it."

Walt hung up and smiled to himself. Bill became clearer to him. It was late in the racing season and Bill hadn't made much and he hadn't done well financially the season before. Walt knew Bill was drawing out of the bank. That first-place check for Bill meant seeing the winter through.

⊰⊱

This is how it had been for Bill Vukovich in those days when the legend was under construction. First a wildly careening young man, then a wildly careening adult, full of internal rages, with a determination so unyielding he seemed to court self-destruction.

Did he do it for money alone?

On many a night if he won it all — fastest qualifying time, a heat, a semifinal, the main event — he might earn $40. He won $10,000 in 1947, when midget racing was in its zenith, but racing had brought him but $500 in that first year, 1938, and $800 the next and $1,100 the third. Then World War II suspended racing.

After that, with his own racer, when the winnings would be all his — along with the traveling expenses and the repairs and the entry fees and the maintenance — he started in again. He was the West Coast midget champion in 1946 and 1947 and the national champion in 1950, with average earnings of less than $7,000 a year. Subtracting the expenses and weighing the result against risk to limb and life, it didn't figure. The best in the nation in 1950, broadening his racing activity past the West Coast and into the Midwest, and yet he was able to make only $450 away from California and he had to draw $1,500 out of the bank that year. And Bill Vukovich was a frugal man. He just raced and went home to the wife and kids.

The same people he warned to stay out of his way or whom he needled about "blowing off" found him an easy man from whom to borrow $50. Or $200. Many paid the money back; those that didn't Bill figured were worth the $50 to be rid of. There was a time when he had $4,000 out in loaned money, and he wasn't sure to whom it all had gone. He, on the other hand, didn't borrow.

All he ever asked for was a push in his midget to get it started. While others worked in elaborate, clean garages on their cars, he would spread a few newspapers on a sidewalk, perhaps in the very shadow of one of those garages, and while dismantling and re-assembling his beloved "Old Ironsides" would predict to his affluent rivals that he was going to blow them off. He would and then laughed at them, but seldom did anyone take umbrage.

In an $800 race at Saugus, he eased into position in the starting field next to Lyle Dickey, the man regarded as having the best chance to win that day. His eyes lit on Dickey's tires. They were pre-war and the wrong tread for this dirt track, but they were all that Dickey had. Bill, in mock anger, yelled to him: "Hey, how the hell do you expect to get anywhere with those crummy tires?" Dickey could only shake his head resignedly.

Muttering a "for Chrissakes," Bill jumped out of his car. Five minutes later he had Dickey's car on tires he himself had brought along in case his own mount had shoe trouble. "Now keep outta my way," he shot at Dickey, "or I'll run right over ya."

He would give advice to a rival and in the next instant regret he was handicapping himself that way but in the third instant would reassure himself: *The hell with it; I'll beat 'em anyway.*

He lent fuel, magnetos and whatever he had extra. He won by combining imagination and brains with nerve. He studied track surfaces and determined what type of tire tread he needed, even if he had to carve in the notches himself. He had a phenomenal record for winning first-of-the-season races. When he saw he was being imitated in tire selection he would mount a fake set — then just before the race, too late for his rivals to follow suit, he would change them. He buffed parts because he couldn't afford to replace them, but he beat everyone, especially enjoying the victories over superior equipment. He put a foot brake in his car to replace the hand lever and, to the amazement of fans, went full speed through turns, unwilling to get off the throttle though others feathered through.

He set track records up and down California. In one week, he went to San Diego, to Los Angeles, to Bakersfield, to Tulare, to Oakland, and then back to Fresno for a day. Sometimes Saugus was included. He left Fresno one morning to drive 600 miles to Phoenix, Arizona, a 12-hour trip, went to bed, arose early, raced in a 100-miler, then started back immediately for Fresno. Jim VanNatta, riding with him, volunteered to relieve. Bill said he would let him know when he grew tired. He never surrendered the wheel.

He was usually first at the track, waiting for the gates to open. He didn't like suggestions from other drivers or mechanics, and when someone in the stands poked fun at his unglamorous "jewel" he usually set the fastest qualifying time. Race over, he was first in the shower.

Solicitous, adoring Mike — his pit manager — would ask him to be less daring: "Iron is easy to get. There's 1,000 pounds of it laying around, so take it careful with yourself." Bill never replied, but playfully poked "Mick" an affectionate blow across the chest.

Once in a crash in Fresno he was hurtled out of the car and into the air and landed on his back, his body spinning sickeningly as he hit. His little girl, Marlene, watching her daddy race for the first time, was among the 9,000 spectators. In that moment many fans unveiled what their real regard was for him. Scores spilled onto the track to rescue him. He was unconscious, with a fractured right hand and brain concussion.

Another time his trousers caught fire from the fuel tank, and he had to abandon the car — but did so reluctantly.

Promoter J.C. Agajanian found him one morning at the track at 5:30. "You've got to get up early to win these races," Bill said. Qualifications began at noon. He took his two laps, sat on the pole with quick time, won the race, collected his money, went home.

There was a special 18-car race one day at Fresno. Six of the classiest Offenhausers, the finest engines in competition, from L.A. were included against Fords, Drakes and more Offys. Bill, with the fast time in his underdog Drake, was moved to the rear for the inverted start. At the very outset someone spun in front of him, forcing him into the infield. He kept steering busily and made his way back to the track, but by this time he was such a poor last the leader was almost on him. As if all this were a movie, he began overtaking the field one by one in a thrilling comeback that brought cheers even from the anti-Vukovich element in the stands. In the final seconds, the crowd standing and cheering in pandemonium, he went by the last man to victory.

In 1941, he won seventeen main events for the pittance of $1,500. In 1946, he could take home nearly that much for a single feature. He put together an unbelievable string of twenty-nine consecutive main event victories. To break the streak, two match races were scheduled. He made it to thirty-one in a row.

✦–✦

Bill had never told Esther why he risked his life racing and she had never pressed him for an explanation. Once a fellow driver had asked him, "What does your wife think about your driving at Indianapolis?" and he had replied, sharply: "I don't know. I never asked her." He had told her about looking through the fence at Fresno to watch his first race when he was a kid and that he decided right then that was it. But that's all the explanation she got.

It was in keeping with his nature. As forcefully as he asserted himself on a racetrack, had been so shy about getting to know Esther Schmidt that even after their initial blind date, for three weeks he'd call her sister and ask her to intercede for him. Finally, Esther confronted him: "See here, Billy Vukovich, if you want me to go out with you, you ask me; don't ask my sister."

Bill still wanted Esther's sister and her companion to join them on dates to help mask his bashfulness until one day he said, with hesitation, "I guess we don't need them anymore, do we?" Esther smiled gently. "No, Billy." A few months later he drove Esther out to the park, parked facing a busy highway, and for a long time said nothing. Then, not looking at Esther, he blurted out: "How would you like to be married to a race driver?" It was all right with her.

He mustered the courage to kiss her and a few days later at the same spot in the park — like countless sentimentalists before him — he gave her a ring.

Bill was racing in San Diego the night Marlene was born in 1941. He got the news at the track, and he suggested to Motter, "Let's get drunk and celebrate after the program." Earl, though disbelieving, smiled an "OK." Bill swept everything that night — fast time, heat, semi, feature, for about $40.

He ordered an unspectacular Tom Collins and had downed only half of it when he stood up to leave. He wanted to hurry home to Fresno. They made it to North Hollywood by 3 a.m. before finally giving in to fatigue. They rented a room and were in bed by 4 a.m. But at 7:30 Earl happened to awaken. There was Bill, shaved, showered, dressed and rocking in a chair, waiting for him.

Bill and Esther were living in Riverside, Calif., in 1944 while he worked for the Army, repairing Jeeps and trucks, when Billy Jr. was born. The proud father stood in front of a mirror in Esther's hospital room and — mindful of the preponderance of girls in the Vukovich bloodlines — kept repeating, "Who said a Vukovich couldn't have a boy?"

What Esther didn't know about the experiences of Bill's childhood — although, coincidentally, they both had lived in Kerman in the Valley during grade school days — she guessed through his treatment of Marlene and Billy. This apparently fearless man who thought nothing of bowling into other race cars at high speed, damn the consequences, couldn't bring himself to spank the children. When disciplining was necessary Bill would ask Esther to apply it and Esther would counter, "That's your job." Bill said, "I can't." Once in a while he'd pat Marlene or Billy on the rump, the extent of his spanking, and Esther would smile and think to herself, *The kids know he's just a big bluff.*

Bill would tell Esther spanking wasn't necessary, that talking to the kids was enough, and Esther would recall Bill's stories of his own father's stinging green switch and absolute, even imperious, authority. Marlene had him charmed, even to the point he would take over her dishwashing chores. Esther sagely let Marlene ask for the money when they went shopping. She knew the take would be bigger.

The kids grew in Bill's image, Marlene exhibiting his vibrancy and little Billy showing his Dad's urge to keep his own counsel and to prefer action over talk.

Bill had started them on an allowance early and increased it gradually over the years. He liked to quote the wealthy Agajanian's advice: "If you take care of the nickels and dimes the dollars will take care of themselves." One day father and son were in the garage, puttering, when Bill offered his son another nickel to add to his allowance. Billy refused. "No, Dad. I have my quarter. That's enough."

Bill went into the house, tremendously pleased, and told Esther. "Now, there's a good kid. He wouldn't take any more." Bill Vukovich himself never wanted more than he was entitled to or had been promised.

Esther knew that the abrupt ending to Bill's childhood when his father committed suicide and his having to work through the Depression years helped shape his determination to get something out of life. But the explanation didn't come from Bill. He said little about his life on the ranch, exhibited no bitterness.

Bill would bring home for Esther odd gifts wrapped carelessly in newspaper — a waste basket or a pencil or some such homely appearing package and he would make a little routine about opening it until Esther grew exasperated. So, one day Bill came in with another package and made no attempt to explain or unveil it. Esther's curiosity overcame her, but Bill refused to open it, telling her she wasn't interested. After much hemming and hawing he tore off the paper. It was a diamond wristwatch. He was secretly romantic (with an expressed appreciation for black negligees) and a hand holder. On a family trip to a drive-in, he wanted Esther to sit close to him as they rode. On nights when they watched television, he would sit with his arm around her.

At times when Bill would attempt to be chummy with Marlene or Billy and they, occupied with something else, wouldn't reciprocate adequately, he would feel rebuffed and announce, "What I need is affection." Esther would answer quietly, "Well, Bill, you have us." And she would think of the little boy in the make-do clothes whipping around the farm and out of his mother's way because she had so many things to do and so many children to worry about.

He would taunt his competitors, ignore his enemies, needle his friends. And the more highly he thought of a person the more he abused him. He seemed incapable of outgoing affection and on close friends like the Motters he heaped sarcasm. But Henrietta Motter accepted this as the reflex of the lack of childhood affection. Not having had any, he didn't know how to give it. Once, at dinner, she got a revealing glimpse of the true Bill Vukovich. He had raced through the meal, as always. Noticing that Henrietta still had food left, he asked her if she intended to finish it. She assured him that she did, and he admonished her to hurry before he swiped some of it. That caused Henrietta to reflect on the struggles of the Vukoviches and understand him better.

Esther would call him on his crustiness and accuse him of having a bark worse than his bite. Motter, having grown from school days into adulthood with him, always felt Bill's heart was bleeding during those times of stress but that he was afraid to let out his emotions.

Moodiness could envelop Vukovich, often for as long as four days. He would sit around the house, looking reflective. Not brooding, just introspect. When Esther asked what bothered him, he would suddenly become alert and reply, "Oh, nothing." Eventually Esther quit trying to pry. She knew he would come out of it. She didn't know how but she knew he would. And yet, when something worried Esther, he would reassure her by saying, "Never you fear, Willie is here."

Bill rarely voiced any feeling of lack, even indirectly. One notable exception was a poignant memory. It was during their days at Riverside. War-time housing scarcity had forced them into one of those demeaning chicken shack apartments that sprouted next to Army camps. They paid $10 a week rent. Bill, a family man barely into his twenties, broke down in bed one night and cried great, bitter tears.

"It won't always be like this," he sobbed to Esther. "We'll have more."

She recognized in him an inferiority complex resulting from his deprived upbringing, which explained some of his avoidance of the public and his often-strained relations with the press. He never sought publicity and shunned the people who could give it to him, to the point of alienating them. Winning would take care of everything. He'd tell Esther: "You blow and go, and they'll write you up. They'll have to."

In his earlier days, when he was not as recognizable and fans would gather around his car in the pits and ask which one was the driver, he'd point to Mike and escape to a shower. He'd stall there while Mike and Eli, if Eli wasn't racing, mounted the car on the trailer and packed while talking with the fans and the press. Once a fan club demonstration at San Diego turned into a mob of 4,000 that tore his clothing in hero worship and unnerved him. He never quite trusted some adults, especially writers. He'd been wary of newspapermen from the early time they'd tagged him, in journalistic parroting, as "The Mad Russian," and had distorted things he'd said.

When Mike one night challenged a sportswriter who had said, "What's the difference? A Russian and a Slav are the same," Bill's antipathy hardened. He hated the "grape picker" tag, too, and tolerated it only with close friends. And he'd always thought he didn't deserve the "villain" designation some newspapermen had put on him. His track opponents considered him unquenchable rather than villainous. With the great majority of reporters, he'd arrived at this uncaring stand: "Write what you want. You don't need me."

3

"We'll put you on Broadway, Bill."

Going to Indianapolis

Bill knew the day would come when he would have to try Indianapolis. He knew it in 1935 when he was 16 and Kelly Petillo won the "500" and he painted Petillo's name on a shed. He still knew it in '48 when Dale Drake, who designed the midget car he drove to so many victories, asked him if he would like to go and he said, "No, that's too fast for me."

He was, in truth, a local legend and local legends have a way of becoming lost, never to rise and be seen again in the giant straightaways and wide, menacing turns of the sprawling ovular arena known as the Indianapolis Motor Speedway.

A legend in automobile racing lasts only when it perpetuates itself at Indianapolis, the big program. Passenger car hot-rods and roadsters are exciting as they lumber along and bump each other. The whining midgets, with their higher pitch, register a thrill, too, for they taunt trouble as exposed drivers, surrounded by a minimum of machinery, wrestle their mounts in and out of one another's orbits. The sprint cars set up dust screens that can blind the driver following and they throw rocks as they skid through turns. They are more dangerous because the machines are faster and heavier.

These races, however, are run on smaller tracks and the challenge is over in minutes. Indianapolis is four hours of all-out big-car speed, of strain, of exposed nerve edges, of vibration and noise and heat, of hurry and chase. Eight hundred turns, all the same way, left, to finish 200 laps and to reach 500 miles. A tense monotony that separates the dedicated

Vukovich's first attempt to qualify for the race was futile. The Maserati "sled" pictured here won the "500" for Wilbur Shaw in 1939 and '40 but was hopelessly outdated by the time it was loaned to him in 1950. (IMS Photos)

from the doubting. The two chutes, north and south, each three-quarters-of-a-mile, present 400 opportunities for a man to force the throttle all the way in if he has the nerve and the confidence to turn with the track, and the skill and luck to keep the car on course and away from the unyielding wall. The turns slant only nine degrees, not enough to thwart centrifugal force. All this with as many as thirty-two others on the track at the same time, challenging with their combinations of speed, nerve, and luck. Who will lift his foot last when the turn must be made?

Bill finally took the plunge into racing's deepest waters in 1950. He arrived in Indianapolis early in May, seeking a ride. But seeking is not always finding at the Speedway. Car owners are cautious with new boys, the good as well as the reckless.

Eventually, though, Bill was asked if he'd like to take a ride in a Maserati. It was one of the most famous cars to ever race at the Speedway, having carried Wilbur Shaw to victory in 1939 and 1940. But this was 1950 and the Maserati was tired, now known as a "sled" among the irreverent new generation at the track. Shaw had won at a 115 mph average, but the qualifying speed now was up to 130.

Bill climbed in, grateful for wheels, and passed his rookie test. Then, after warming up, he urged the tired old warhorse to 126 mph — two mph faster than anyone else had been able to make it go. But, strangely, its owner wheeled it into the garage and let it sit.

That evening, Bill decided to relax a little. He dropped in at the tavern where drivers and mechanics hung out. The day's activities at the track got a review, then the needle came out. Suddenly the hard-driving Johnnie Parsons said: "Go home, Vuky; you don't want to go that fast."

Bill blanched. His lips tightened and his jaw worked. Without a word, he stood and left. And he did go home. All the way to Fresno.

➵➴

Vukovich knew there was no point in sticking around and hoping to be offered another car to qualify for the race. It was unlikely a faster one would turn up needing a pilot, and even less likely that it would go to a rookie if it did.

He also knew it would be unbearable to watch others race, so he spent the next year grinding his teeth in California and storing his wrath against the day he could spit it out lap by lap for 500 miles.

Occasionally he eased his tension with a midget race, but the miniature dervishes had begun to lose their crowd appeal and the programs dwindled. It was in this year Bill could manage only $450 in winnings and he had to withdraw $1,500 of the savings he and Esther had scraped together.

May, 1951, finally came and he headed to Indianapolis again to answer an insult and overcome a mental block.

He cleared the first hurdle, landing a ride in a new car owned by Pete Salemi of Cleveland. It was a tired "turtle" — the Central Excavating Special — but at least he had something to drive that was capable of making the race.

On one practice run a radius rod broke loose and dangled perilously. In such situations drivers usually shut off the engine, reach for the brake and stop as quickly as possible. Bill kept his speed, calmly reached for the rod, held the loose end in his hand, returned to the pits with his other hand steering and yelled to his mechanic: "Hey, come fix this damned thing!"

That raised eyebrows in the pits and car designer Bill Stroppe turned to a mechanic who'd made a few disparaging remarks about Bill in the past. "What did you say about this boy?" Stroppe asked. The mechanic was notably silent.

Bill qualified. He knew he couldn't be competitive in the "sled," but he would push it for all it had in it, which he thought would be about thirty laps.

Indianapolis newspapers, despite the reams of space they devote to the race, didn't know anything about him and his name appeared only in lineups. In one pre-qualification story he was not listed among seventeen drivers and cars predicted capable of 132 mph. He did 133.725. One paper ran a form chart and listed him at 50-1 odds to win the race, the least favored in the field along with two other drivers. The official program spelled it "Vukovitch."

Although incapable of running with the leaders, Vukovich's car was at least capable of qualifying for the 1951 race and enabled him to show off his talent. He started twentieth and was running in tenth place when an oil leak forced him out after twenty-nine laps. The newspapers didn't always spell his name correctly but he caught the eye of the right people. (IMS Photos)

He started in twentieth position. Somewhere, somehow, he put enough of himself into a second-rate car to have it running in tenth by the first fifty miles — twenty laps. He was still tenth on the twenty-ninth lap when the car quit. Oil trouble. Before he dropped out, he had made it into the lead story of race-day newspaper editions, a far jump from the 50-1 odds previously accorded him. The Central Excavating Special was awarded twenty-ninth place, with winnings of $750.

He had done well with a hopeless car. Twenty-ninth place was galling to the man who couldn't accept second place, but others had seen enough.

The day after the race he received a telephone call.

"This is Stu Hilborn. Who are you going to drive for next year?"

"Hell, I don't know," Bill replied. "That's a year away."

"Well, don't do anything definite," Hilborn said. "We think we're going to build a rear drive for next year and we think Rose is probably ready to retire. So, we'd like you to keep it in mind."

Hilborn was speaking for the Howard Keck organization, an established combination of money and talent at the Speedway. Keck's millions — he was an oilman — gave free reign to two precocious chief mechanics, Jim Travers and Frank Coon, and Hilborn, who was developing a fuel injection he wanted to introduce to racing. The great Mauri Rose, twice a "500" winner and once a co-winner, had been their man in the '51 race, but Rose went scraping overturned in a ditch when a wheel collapsed. He emerged unhurt, but this had been Rose's fifteenth straight "500" and he did a lot of thinking while he was upside down, hunched in the cockpit, grinding along on his head, his life dependent solely on the whim of a berserk automobile.

→-←

Vukovich wanted to face full square the Indianapolis challenge, and so he curtailed the midget grind. He did a lot of thinking, much of it about his family and the severity of the 500-Mile Race, with its dangers not lost on him. There was a closeness growing now between him and the children through incidents that delighted him. He sought to provide them with comforts and playthings that had been denied him but only through a program of discipline in which they first proved themselves worthy. They responded, to his pleasure, by sometimes demanding more of themselves than he did.

He had made a loose agreement with another Indianapolis car owner before Hilborn asked him to consider driving for the Keck team in 1952 and he fretted about that through the fall and winter in Fresno, wondering if and when a firm offer would come. It finally came in February, via a phone call from Travers, who added they were building a front drive.

"What happened to the rear drive you were going to build?" Bill asked. He knew rear drives were becoming more popular with their superior power and improved handling. Travers said the Keck group thought it would try it with a front drive again. So, nothing was decided between them. Bill was left to fret some more, uncertain what to do in light of his other offer.

Not much later, Travers called again. They were going to build a rear drive after all. Bill said OK, and Travers ended the conversation with a lighthearted prediction: "We'll put you on Broadway, Bill, with our know-how and equipment."

Just like that, the right driver and the right mechanics and the right equipment and the right car owner had merged at the same intersection. The team would come to be known as the "Keck Kids," or, sarcastically, as the "Check Kids" or the "Rich Kids."

Bill's first phone call was to the other owner with whom he'd talked about driving, telling him of his decision to join Keck so that another pilot could be obtained. Then, he signed a contract with Keck, a first for him. Having always regarded a man's word as sufficient, this formal business arrangement felt alien to him.

◆-◆

He promised Billy Jr. that if he would quit biting his fingernails for a month before it came time to leave for Indianapolis, he would give him $10. Billy resisted the temptation for the necessary month, and Bill handed over the $10. Billy Jr. wanted to buy "a hundred comic books," but Daddy vetoed that idea. Shortly before Bill was to leave for Indianapolis, Billy Jr. asked to speak to him in his room.

"Tell me out here, son," Dad said. Esther was with them in the living room.

Billy swallowed. "OK … Daddy, if you need that $10 to go to Indianapolis, I'll give it back to you."

Bill paused. Gently, he replied: "No, son. If I needed it, I wouldn't have given it to you in the first place."

Touched, he walked out of the room. Two days later he left Fresno for his mission nearly 2,500 miles away. By then he had slipped into his hard, steely exterior. No one else was going to get the view Esther, Marlene, and Billy Jr. got.

4

"What a dirty, lousy break!"

A Close Scrape

Vukovich and the Keck crew came quietly to Indianapolis in 1952 and worked unobtrusively. But something special was taking shape behind their garage door.

The mechanical aptitude of Travers and Coon was enhanced by their smooth partnership. Both had gone into the service immediately after high school graduation in southern California. Travers wound up at Iwo Jima. While stationed there, he built a midget race car using two cylinders from a Japanese jeep. Longtime friends, the two advanced in racing in the same sequence as the drivers — the hot rods, then the midgets, and on up. Travers was volatile, spoke up; Coon was phlegmatic, spoke seldom.

They were young and ambitious and unafraid to pioneer while Keck gave them free rein and an open checkbook. They built their new car for Indianapolis in six weeks.

It was unconventional. The body was of the latest Kurtis Kraft design, but it was simpler and lighter. And, in a daring move, they tilted the Offenhauser engine on a 36-degree angle to the left, with crankshaft and driveshaft also running in unorthodox fashion on the left side. They reasoned this would help hold the weight to the inside in turns, thus improving handling and speed. With the driveshaft on one side the driver could also sit lower, lowering the center of gravity. In time this type of Speedway car was to be called a "roadster." Torsion bars were mounted crossways instead of longitudinal as in the past. They installed

Hilborn's jet injectors. Most race car designers were beginning to see the wisdom of his idea because they provided a more consistent fuel feed than the usual manifold carburetion system that could be erratic.

They called the sleek, gray automobile — numbered 26 — the Fuel Injection Special. It weighed 1,625 pounds, below average. But in it sat a muscular man with a heavy throttle foot, weighted by determination.

Vukovich considered the 500-Mile Race an athletic contest. He rode a bicycle for miles around Fresno throughout the off-season and made pushups and calisthenics part of his daily routine. He squeezed a hard rubber ball to keep his fingers and forearms strong. And he walked and walked. Arms and legs and wind. Let the others wait until May to arrive at Indianapolis and perhaps take a few minutes on a steering-wheel mockup or run around the garage area or hunt up a gymnasium for a short visit or two.

He smoked an occasional cigar, mostly for laughs. He didn't smoke enough of them to know how to carry them off without attracting attention. Drinking was still something someone else did.

He continued to avoid people in general and newspaper and radio men in particular. But he would loosen up a bit with Travers and Coon, needling them about the car, and would chat with Agajanian, whom he admired, and exchange banter with fellow drivers Faulkner and Tony Bettenhausen, both expert garage "lawyers." But to others he was just a man walking by.

Besides, the public's attention this year was elsewhere. It focused primarily on the radical Cummins Diesel, with its excessive weight and truck engine, driven by Freddie Agabashian. There also was the Italian Ferrari, lending international flavor, with the world-renowned driver Alberto Ascari trying Indianapolis for the first time. The Novis, the two brutes with the unharnessed speed and a seven-year trail of death, fire, and other mishaps always drew attention, as did popular driver Jack McGrath.

Two days before the first weekend of qualifying, Vukovich whirled through several practice laps in the high 136s. The Kecks had posted their notice.

✦—✦

Qualifications arrived on a cold, overcast day, bringing 70,000 spectators. McGrath ran a lap at 136.664 mph, the second-fastest time in Speedway history. Andy Linden followed with a record four-lap average of 137.002. George Connor, traveling 165 mph down the home stretch, maintained the throng's interest by spinning and sliding backwards 1,700 feet, miraculously hitting nothing. With only a few minutes left in the day, Agabashian took the ponderous Diesel out and clicked off his ten miles in 138.010. It was a new record and the pole position for the oil burner, the odd duck in the flock. One tire on the 2,480-pound beast finished in ribbons.

Meanwhile, the Keck crew had a balky new machine on their hands they weren't prepared yet to try. Keck, on the phone from Los Angeles, advised Travers to give up on the car but Jim said no, he had some more ideas.

Practice resumed and the Novi reclaimed the spotlight with an unofficial 140 mph lap under the hand of Chet Miller. This was the dream speed everyone had waited for.

The soft-voiced, veteran Miller was one of the few rivals who had Vukovich's ear. After one practice session, Bill, dissatisfied with his progress, sought him out. Miller, regarded as having the most rhythmical technique around the Indianapolis oval, advised him to ride a little higher in the groove. Bill tried the new path and later credited Chet with giving him an extra five miles per hour.

As practice continued, some of the savants sitting in the curves clocking turn speed sent word that Vukovich was negotiating the course exceptionally fast, a clue to a possible fast time trial run.

The second qualifying weekend brought a forecast predicting rain might hold off on Saturday but would surely fall on Sunday. Time was now short. By the 11 a.m. start there was a long line of cars waiting. The Fuel Injection was at the head of it, although the Kecks didn't really feel ready.

It had rained earlier, but now was partly cloudy. Only 5,000 faithful fans were in the stands. Most were anticipating the appearance of Miller's

Novi and other cars and there was no stir when the relatively unknown Bill Vukovich was pushed to the apron in relative obscurity.

His second lap was 139.427 and the public address announcer had to repeat the speed pointedly to awaken the crowd into realizing that he had just set a one-lap record, breaking Agabashian's week-old 139.104. Bill went on to post a four-lap mark at 138.212. He looked bewildered as he arrived in his pit and his crew shouted above the crowd noise, "Hey, you broke 'em all!"

Still stunned, Bill finally told Travers, "It felt sloppy."

Thirty minutes later, back in the garage, he looked up and asked his crew: "Hey, did we set a four-lap record?" Success did not dawn easy on him.

Eventually he lit a cigar and got settled in a chair in the privacy of the garage with Travers and Coon, and with hand gestures dispensed a mixture of dry wit and philosophy.

"Well, anyway, maybe we won't get bumped," he said wryly. Travers kidded him: "If we hadn't put those big throttle springs on you might have got on it more." Bill didn't bother to answer that; it had been obvious how deep down the chutes he had stayed on the throttle.

Bill went on. "You get all excited around here. I was talking to myself until I hit that short north straightaway, 'get on this damn thing!' ... You know, the 139 lap felt the smoothest of all. When you get excited you get sloppy. I went wide on my last two laps."

Then, realistically, "Records are made to be broken. The Novi will probably beat us later on."

"The Novi will take away the happiness, all right," Travers agreed, "But we've got it for a while. That's more than some have had."

Coon continued to work silently and carefully around the car, seeing that it was buttoned and covered.

A few friends had now arrived and to one of them Bill said, "The guys have worked their tail off to get us ready."

Travers couldn't let slip this rare moment of sincerity from Vukovich. Straight-faced, he heckled: "We give you a good car, and you go out and sluff off. Keck called and he wanted to know why you didn't go faster."

Bill shot back: "Tell him we've got a helmet that will just fit him.

"It's getting to be around here like the midgets used to be," he added. "Someday they'll be driving around here full throttle all the way around."

As the weather improved, 50,000 eventually filed into the stands and the Novi, with Miller, did in fact steal some of the Vukovich crew's glory with a one-lap record of 139.600 before a fused piston halted the attempt. The erasure of the Keck marks became complete when Miller, in a second try, made the four laps in 139.034. Bettenhausen then made more news when he hit the wall and wiped out the car that had won the race the year before, the Belanger 99.

But for a moment — and one day's edition of the newspapers — Vukovich had sent reporters hunting up the Speedway's biography cards. He had made it into a headline, as if he cared, and now race fans outside of California could mispronounce his name and wonder where this new headliner had come from.

I decided it was time, despite Vukovich's aversion to newspapermen, to ask some questions. I thought it best to have Agajanian, for whom Vukovich had a high regard, to make the introductions and pave the way for the interview. The idea worked. Bill, wanting to oblige his friend, held still, leaning against a bleacher wall, answering quietly, respectfully. Aggie remained on hand to help him feel comfortable.

Did he call his family after his record run? "Naw. I figured they'd read the papers."

What can the car do? "I know damn well the car will go 140."

How about the race? Would he attempt to go to the front in a hurry? "I'm gonna wait a few laps and see what the others are going to do. If a guy can make some lap money, why shouldn't he?"

Any superstitions? "Aw, crap!"

The salty language increased and Bill began to loosen a bit. For some inexplicable reason the conversation turned to the subject of conceit, injected by Agajanian to draw out Vukovich. In one expressive gesture Bill stated his position about his headline speed and registered his displeasure with those who had let fame enlarge their egos.

"Big-headed people!" he sneered, moving open hands back and forth from the sides of his head. "I figure if these peasants can set records, so can I."

Then, with a touch of sarcasm: "Let's start a 138-Mile-an-Hour Club. (He was referring to the recently formed 135-Mile-an-Hour Club, for qualifiers of that speed.) Then I can be a wheel for a year."

It was a moment of some incongruity, as if Bill Vukovich, son of immigrants and new boy in this glamorous big-car company at Indianapolis, was saying, "I'm as good as anyone here."

He asked obligingly if he had provided all the information wanted. Assured he had, he hastened to his garage.

※

The night before the race the Keck Kids were pessimistic. They didn't think their car was capable enough. They decided to run "flat out" until a pit stop was needed and thus force their competitors to stay with them and pit after Bill would. He agreed.

The cars were lined up the day of the race in typically great Speedway weather — fair and cool, with a little breeze. Meanwhile, the Hollywood actress was ensconced in the exclusive Pagoda, to wait through the four hours of the race until she was taken to the Bullpen at the end of the pits to kiss the winner and usurp his moment, as is the 500-Mile Race custom. This year it was Arlene Dahl.

Bill was in the eighth position, in the middle of the third row. Troy Ruttman was on his left, Cliff Griffith to his right. Agabashian was on the pole, McGrath in his usual outside-front row spot. Duke Nalon, in one Novi, was inside second row. Three years before, a Novi had carried Nalon into the wall, exploded, skidded backwards along the cement, and left him badly burned. Ascari was in the seventh row. Miller, the 49-year-old dean of the active drivers, was deep in the ninth section because, despite his record time trial, he had done it on the last day of qualifications. (The lineup is determined not only by speed, but also by order.)

The Indianapolis News race form had placed McGrath the favorite to win at 5-1 odds, Vukovich at 6-1, the Miller-Nalon entry and Ascari at 7-1, Ruttman 12-1. Of Vukovich, for whom it had changed from 50-1 to 6-1 in only a year, it read: "Highly respected driver, new car is geared for action, as was demonstrated when it set a new four-lap record in qualifying. Should be among the toppers in race." Of McGrath: "The favorite. Might have won last year. Car appears in perfect condition, driver is tops. Will take some doing to beat him." Of Ruttman, in Agajanian's No. 98: "Great possibilities. Fast car, driver knows track. Determination is hallmark of garage. Someday they'll do it."

At the end of the first lap, it was McGrath in front, Jim Rathmann two lengths behind, followed by Ruttman, Duane Carter, Nalon, Vukovich.

After two laps: McGrath, Ruttman, Rathmann and Vukovich.

Third lap: McGrath, Ruttman and Vukovich.

Fourth lap: McGrath, Vukovich.

Fifth lap: McGrath, Vukovich.

Sixth lap: Vukovich.

Bill Vukovich had arrived at Indianapolis. As he passed the pits, he waved to his crew, "OK."

The pace he set was record breaking. After ten laps — twenty-five miles — it was 132.538, far superior to the previous standard of 128.249 set by McGrath the year before. But Ruttman was fighting back. In the twelfth lap he put his grill in front of Vukovich. Bill threw the challenge back into Troy's teeth — and jumped two seconds in front. He stayed there. Slowly, he built his lead. He passed others where he found them, taking whichever course or adding whatever speed he needed, disregarding risk. In the main straightaway on the eighteenth lap he fled past a traffic snarl by taking to the inside of the track.

He was twenty-nine seconds ahead of Ruttman after sixty laps but on the sixty-second he had to make a pit stop — the first he had ever made at Indianapolis. He executed perfectly. The Keck crew gave him four tires and fuel in 1 minute, 29 seconds. Ruttman, still racing, shot into the lead. Bill sat calmly during the stop, but his lips were tight. He then went after Troy, who was moving at a record 131.149. Now it was Ruttman's turn for pit repairs. He chose Lap 83 — and Bill went flying by, first again.

A brush with tragedy hit the Ruttman pit. Gasoline spilled onto the hot exhaust pipe and instantly flames leaped above Troy's head. Mechanic Clay Smith threw himself across the strapped-in-driver, taking the burns on his exposed arm. Troy's father, part of his crew, was burned around the eyes. Firemen quickly starved the blaze in carbon dioxide, but it took two minutes to return Ruttman to the track. As he went into gear Troy waved a clenched fist to the crowd. Rathmann was now second. The race began to assume a semblance of order.

At halfway — 250 miles, 100 laps — based on speed alone the race was between Vukovich, Rathmann and Ruttman. But Rathmann had made his first pit stop too early and would have to stop twice more. And Ruttman wasn't likely to pick up the ninety-seven seconds by which he trailed Vukovich.

The Keck Fuel Injection Special purred on faithfully. On Lap 112 Bill held aloft thumb and forefinger for his crew. Everything OK. By the 120th he had won $9,300 in lap money, at $100 a lap. At 128 Ruttman's was the only car within three laps of him and Troy trailed by a lap and forty-three seconds. Rathmann had pitted and now was third. The race was settling down, but not Vukovich; pushing himself, he still was passing people in turns. The pace continued, three mph faster than the previous standard. Now, two hours into the race, the weather conditions were perfect for setting records.

Bill chose Lap 135 for his second and final stop, but the excited crew mounted the right rear tire backwards and had to do it all over. The service, three clean tires (the left front still had tread) and water for the driver, consumed 2 minutes, 8 seconds — and the lead was reclaimed by Ruttman.

Vukovich, furious, cut four seconds off Ruttman's 40-second lead in the 138th lap alone, and Troy still had his second stop to make. In eight more laps Bill had trimmed the margin to thirty seconds. Troy came in on Lap 148 and the Agajanian crew fashioned a sensational 56-second change for him — but Bill had roared past.

Arlene Dahl and her entourage started for the Victory Bullpen. Esther Vukovich prepared to leave her seat and go as well. Bill was sailing now, feeding his hunger. At the 450-mile post he was still running an unprecedented 133 mph and staying thirty seconds in front of Ruttman. Only twenty more laps. Every minute and 7 seconds, one more was clicked off.

Suddenly, Bill felt a strange reaction from the steering wheel. Something was wrong. He was out of the straightaway and into a turn, but the wheel wouldn't turn properly. He twisted it hard left, biceps popping.

The next turn was worse. The one after that worse still. Each curve, he had to take a bit wider. Could he stay on the track for just enough laps to finish all 200 — and at the same time hold off Ruttman?

Vukovich began fighting his lonely, desperate battle, wrestling fate at every turn, struggling for enough turning radius. Ruttman was gaining a second a lap, but the throng of 175,000, unaware of Bill's dilemma and long since having conceded Vukovich victory, didn't figure Troy to close the gap. With ten laps left, twenty-two seconds separated them.

The Keck Kids secured their pit equipment so they could make the two-block walk to the Bullpen and the victory celebration in time to receive Bill when he drove in. It had been a nerve-wracking four hours.

Bill got through the 191st lap, started his 192nd. Turning now was torture. He got through the southwest corner, straightened out through the short south stretch, headed into the second turn. He made a sweep almost as wide as the track itself, perilously close to the cement retaining wall. As he came out of the bend the steering wheel went rigid.

He knew victory was gone. His immediate concern now was his peril. He was in a car flying nearly 130 mph with no ability to turn and he had less than the three-quarter-mile straightaway in which to save himself before reaching the third turn, because he was unable to keep the car on a straight path.

But stubborn, uncompromising man that he was, he refused to lift his foot, hoping to bully the car into obeying. It wouldn't. He bolted at an angle toward the hub-high railing enclosing the backstretch, and it scared him. He eased off now and grudgingly touched brake, so he wouldn't wreck the car and himself, but when he entered the third turn, he was still going 90 mph and headed for the wall. He gave a desperate yank to the left and luckily the slope of the banked corner helped turn his wheels. He scraped along the wall, dust and cement chips flying, women screaming, official observers fleeing, as he ground 350 feet to a

Vukovich was just eight laps from his first "500" victory in 1952 when a broken 50-cent cotter pin caused his steering wheel to malfunction and forced him into the third-turn wall. His only consolation was that he proved to himself – and others - he could win the race. (Bob Gates collection)

stop. He was little more than eight laps — just nine minutes — from first place and its prize of $61,743. That fell to Ruttman.

Vukovich lifted himself out of the car, unhurt, vigorously snapping his right arm up and down in uncontrollable disgust. He walked around the car shaking his head. He placed one foot on the wall, hands on hips, faced the car, track, and sympathetic throng in the infield, eyes blazing, consumed with rage.

When the car hit the wall the yellow warning lights were instantly switched on. The Keck crew, including Howard Keck himself, stood searching up track, disbelieving. No. 26 hadn't come around. Esther, too, had counted off the cars and she hurried to the hospital. The public address shouted frantic drama, reporting the abrupt twist of fate that had turned Vukovich's certain victory into calamity. The race concluded at a slackened, anticlimactic pace.

Bill was oblivious to the hub bub around him. He set out for the garage area, nearly a mile away. The ambulance and its doctor and nurse had caught up with him now and pleaded with him to accompany them to the hospital. He ignored them, walking swiftly away as they followed him.

Ruttman was in the Bullpen, admitting in his first flush of triumph, "I couldn't catch Billy."

During that agonizing walk back to the garages a realization penetrated Vukovich's anger and frustration. Not enough to soothe him, for it was merely a pebble thrown into a tornado, but it did come to him. So, this was Indianapolis? Why the fear of speed in the bigger cars that he had expressed to Drake? What had he been worried about? What had he been waiting for? And why the greater fear, the one he kept to himself? That he might not be able to win? Hadn't he all but won this one?

But when he strode through the doors of Garage No. 11, awaited by a devastated crew, he unleashed his wrath again, directing it at the automobile that had carried him for nearly 192 laps but couldn't quite manage eight more. He called on nearly every swear word he knew, drawing from a deep lode. Travers and Coon, too, were angry, but more at the fates than at the failed racing machine, which they had so painstakingly pieced together. A broken cotter pin, they discovered, had caused the steering failure — a clamp that could be bought for 50 cents.

Bill continued his tirade. "What a dirty, lousy break! That Ruttman never won an easier one!"

As he raved, a concerned doctor and nurse asked the crew, "Don't you think we should take him to the hospital? He's out of his head." They replied, "Wouldn't you be if you'd just lost all that money?" Keck — who once had been disappointed to see his driver wave to his wife during the pace lap, doubting his concentration — watched silently and knew he now had a boy who wanted to win badly enough.

For two hours Bill unburdened himself, often by savagely kicking his helmet across the garage floor. Finally, he turned abruptly to Travers and spoke more calmly, "It's a cinch. I should have been here ten years ago!"

The next night at the Victory Dinner, Ruttman, who had led forty-four laps, was awarded the winner's check of $61,743. Vukovich, who had led 153 and finished seventeenth, earned $18,693. Throughout the long payoff ceremony, with introductions and responses, Bill sat wordlessly, usually staring at the ceiling, thoughtfully.

Master of ceremonies Lee Wallard, the 1951 winner, offered condolences when it was Vukovich's turn to come up and receive his check.

"Something like this is hard to take, but I always say these things happen for the best," Wallard said. "We do have our boy Bill with us tonight."

As Bill made his way to the microphone, Bettenhausen stood and started clapping. The banquet crowd of 600 immediately stood and tendered Bill the greatest applause of the evening. This was the first time in memory a standing ovation had been given to anyone but the winner. Bill reached for his pay envelope, said "Thanks," and returned to his seat.

He was gazing at the ceiling again when Ruttman, receiving his winner's share, said, "Don't ever let anybody tell you that Vukovich can't go, because he can, and I can tell you."

Vukovich and Ruttman, both smiling, posed for newspaper photographers afterward comparing their checks. Later, however, a newspaper reporter with sodden manners and appalling inaccuracy, accused Bill of crashing because of fatigue. Wallard and Bettenhausen calmed him and advised the reporter to leave.

The next day, Bill Vukovich went back to Fresno to brood.

5

"If you want someone to run second for you, get yourself another boy!"

Recover, Regroup, Return

Back home, he started to tell 8-year-old Billy about the race. Billy cut him off: "Yeh, I know all about it; you crashed." Then he went on about the business of being a cowboy, not a race driver.

Big Bill moped around the house for a while thinking of the race. It was the only time Esther had known him to be bitter. Eventually, she thought he gained satisfaction from knowing he was capable of winning, but the challenge remained, more taunting than ever.

He *hadn't* won and he didn't know of the existence of moral victories. The public did, however. The tale of Bill Vukovich's heartbreak, when the knob of the door to success had come off in his hand, grew and with retelling fixed him as the unofficial winner and a man worthy of sympathy.

This feeling became so firmly rooted within the racing clan that the renowned Ralph DePalma, usually an impeccably gracious individual, made jest of Vukovich's luck in an occasional speaking engagement. Hadn't Vukovich won $18,000? And hadn't he, DePalma, come closer in 1912, within just two laps of winning, when he was ten miles — four laps — in front? And been paid nothing, because only the first ten were paid?

Vukovich rejected the martyr's role. He refused the comfort of commiseration and instead prepared again for the test. Though he had at least outwardly accepted the role of villain given him by the midget crowds, a designation he couldn't understand, he cared not for sympathy.

He returned to the midget trail and in the middle of the summer when an accident put Ruttman on the shelf, he accepted Agajanian's offer to drive the latter's car on the dirt-track circuit.

The last event of the season — it was to be Bill's final "big car" competition other than Indianapolis — was at San Jose. Bobby Ball, obviously in the best equipment, held a substantial lead. Bill, second, had no chance to catch him. Runner-up was a cinch, but he was determined to overtake Ball. Round and 'round he chased, driving at the ragged edge. It was too much for the car. He spun out.

An angry Agajanian rushed up and berated him for not playing it safe and collecting certain second-place money.

Bill slammed his helmet to the ground.

"Listen, you sonavabitch!" he spat. "If you want someone to run second for you, get yourself another boy!"

On his off days, Bill straddled his English racer bicycle and rode for miles around Fresno's level terrain. If he hadn't had an out-of-town race the night before, he would wake up between 4 and 6 in the morning and take a long walk or ride his bike.

He lifted weights, did fingertip pushups, skipped rope, punched a light bag. He squeezed remarkably stiff hand grippers — each a V-shaped coiled spring with wooden handles at their most difficult setting — while watching television until the clicking noise drove the rest of his family to protest. He maintained a disciplined diet, too, and avoided parties.

"I'll show those guys the way," he told his family. "They'll have to get up awfully early to beat Willy."

Meanwhile, south of Fresno in Los Angeles, Travers and Coon went about the tedium of reassembling the automobile, rearranging the combination with the hope that it would hold up for 500 miles rather than 480. The easy-going, husky Coon manipulated the engine with the exactitude of a surgeon while the smaller, sometimes volatile Travers labored long over the chassis. Goaded by the letdown of the steering pin, they heat-treated every part and checked it for hardness. They mounted all new parts around the steering apparatus.

Not far away a close friend and rival, mechanic Herb Porter, exhorted his own crew throughout the winter: "The Keck Kids are flying. You gotta beat Vuky, you gotta beat Vuky."

The same feeling spread around California, where much of the big car racing fraternity hibernates until once again Indiana is blossoming and it's time to hitch the trailer and point toward Indianapolis.

By May 1953, Vukovich's near-miss in '52 had made him a formidable figure. But he felt himself a failure. The eleven months had done little to alleviate the frustration. Fame and sympathy had barely eased his exasperation. He returned to Indianapolis to begin a month of stalking a prize that had been all but his, a prize often bulwarked by death, for twenty-two drivers had died at the Speedway seeking it.

✦✦

May is a lovely month in Indiana, fragrant with reawakening earth, newly painted green and full of fresh bloom against a backdrop of blue sky. But few mechanics at the Indianapolis Speedway notice it. They're aware only of whatever weather manages to come through the garage doors or of whatever carburetion changes the atmosphere forces them to make. Travers and Coon unloaded the blue iron steed and began grooming it.

Bill walked and fretted and needled. He boarded again with Lawrence and Dorcas Thompson in Speedway City, a half-mile from the track's main gate and a mile from his garage. He hiked the distance often, while others rode. Every morning he rolled out of bed early, dropped to the floor, did pushups — fifteen, twenty, twenty-five. In the evening if he was too exhausted to exercise before flopping into bed, he'd lecture himself — *Willpower is going to win this race.* Then he would be back on the floor, strengthening shoulder and arm muscles.

His moods shifted often, but as the big day, the 30th, approached, he grew more introspective, increasingly edgy, and restless.

On the 11th of May, he turned the Fuel Injection Special at 138.1 mph, the fastest practice lap to date, sending word that he was back to finish the job this time. The Keck Kids had given the other garages — eighty-three cars were entered for the '53 race — a hint at the speed they'd best try for, and they left many a mechanic and driver exasperated and frustrated. They set a goal of 135 for qualification.

Before the month was out Bill was to call that wonderful little machine of his "turtle," "hog," "pig," and several more earthy names, insulting it to hide his admiration.

On a cold, rainy May 13th, Vukovich, Travers, Coon and Hilborn were holed up in their garage where they alternately needled each other and worked on the car, ceaselessly checking and tinkering. Travers and Coon were trying to determine the clearance between the housing set screws and a frame post.

They found the holes not too far off from each other but 500-thousandths of an inch off the set screws. They fretted and measured and re-measured, until finally Bill broke in: "Now, wait a minute. You guys are getting too damned technical with your half-a-thousandths and 500-thousandths crap. When we get to running you know damned well that magnesium will grow. That damned stuff grows more than aluminum when it gets hot, so it'll come out all right if you leave a little play in it now."

Bill shouted it, as was often his habit, curly head bobbing, gold fillings flashing. His technical understanding of a racing machine, as keenly developed as his talent for driving one, was well known to Travers and Coon. They listened — and agreed that it might be wise to let the play in the housing remain.

There was a clipping from a Los Angeles newspaper on the wall about Ruttman, in which Troy told what he had thought while chasing Vukovich: *Go ahead, Vuky, you're a rough kid on tires. I'll get you later.* One paragraph, circled by the Keck Kids, quoted Ruttman: "I knew I could catch Vuky. He was slowing down. When I came out of the pits, I was fifty-five seconds behind and when he crashed, I was only seventeen seconds behind."

I read the article after visiting the garage, then turned to Bill and informed him of what Ruttman had said only minutes after the race: "I couldn't catch Billy."

Bill snorted: "Everybody knows damned well he couldn't have caught me."

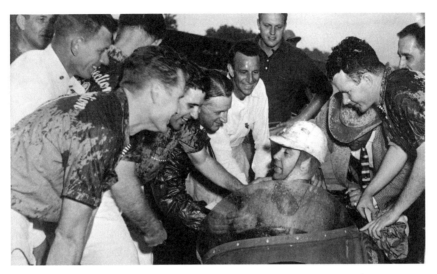

Vukovich, soaked by a sudden rainstorm, accepts congratulations after completing the dramatic qualifying run that landed him on the pole. (IMS Photos)

Travers cut in, mockingly polite: "Now, Bill, we must be good sports in this racing business. You know we're in this for the sport of it, not to make money or anything."

"Crap!"

"The only guy in this garage in this for the sport of it is this guy Keck." Travers said it respectfully. "I never knew anyone like him. He didn't do a bit of squawking about last year. He said he didn't want to hear a thing about it. He wanted no publicity. Just said, 'forget it' and it just made him more determined to come back here and win the damned race."

"Well, it's easy for him to be a good sport with his money," Bill said, but quickly pivoted.

"I never knew a guy who had so much money who said so little. He just stands back in the corner and doesn't say a damn thing … only once … he came in here last year just before the race and he says to the guys, 'How are we going to run the race; what are our plans?' I says, 'Balls, we'll either get out in front and run ahead or we'll just have to follow the rest' … that's all the damned plans we had."

Bill began rambling, moving from the pit difficulties of last year to the steering mishap and then to his fortunate assignment to drive the Keck car. "I'm not kidding myself. I try to be honest with myself, see. I'll tell you why I got into this car — they just couldn't get anybody else."

Then he launched into a confession about having told the Keck Kids a cock-and-bull story about a hot, new car Agajanian had signed him to for $5,000, trying to negotiate a fatter contract.

"The guys wanted to know why I was leaving them, and I told them all this crap," he said. "I kept needling them, trying to get a better offer, see — silly thing I do. Hell, I was driving for the best guy in the business, great equipment, smart mechanics … anyway, I finally told Hilborn, and Travers — ole Crabby; I call him Crabby 'cause he's hot-headed and always bitching — ole Crabby comes in, see, and he'd been overhearing and he was grinning … and I figure if a guy can drive for forty percent, which I got, there's not more he can go up, see, so …"

Travers and Hilborn listened in good-natured silence. A voice broke in: "You're so damned independent. You always have been."

"I am not independent. I've just always paid my way. There are useless bastards who are too damned lazy to work … if their old man quit working tomorrow, they'd starve to death. I've given guys money I've never seen. Hell, I bought a guy a car; hell, two of them. But think I ever see anything from them?"

It was building in Vukovich now. The useless, rainy days like this one are the worst. Race drivers fret more then, and he had arrived already worked up.

Out of the rain came little Faulkner, to visit. Walt was having difficulty finding more speed. It was Faulkner who cracked the Speedway "sonic" barrier with his 136-mile-an-hour lap in his rookie year, 1951, that gave subsequent drivers the courage to "stand on it" practically all the way around the track. In a flash he and Bill generated a high dudgeon. Shouting, at three paces, they spilled out their anxiety and impatience, trying to expunge their uneasiness with the swearing characteristic of their breed of racing man.

Walt sounded bitter. "Why a guy would ever want to be a race driver! I'd give anything to have a job, punch the damned time clock at 9 in the morning, knock off at 5, go home to the little woman and kids, eat a good supper, turn on the damned TV set, go to bed, get up and go to work at 9!"

Someone in a corner asked slyly: "Why don't you do it?" Before Walt could answer, Bill cut in:

"This damned race driver business. I'm no goddamned race driver. To be honest with you I'm too damn lazy to get a damned job and work. So, I'm driving race cars!"

Neither meant it, of course. Race drivers seldom mention, or at least they downplay, the romanticism of their calling. And it gets pretty awful, the waiting around.

But better weather followed, and cars took to the track in steady day-long streams, each outfit looking for the right combination of driving technique, chassis suspension, spark, mixture, weight transfer. Vukovich, now the hare, merely took an occasional teaser lap, but mostly he just visited and sat for a daily five-minute turn on a steering-wheel mock-up in the garage area. And did his pushups. And walked and walked. His 5-foot-8 frame now had only 160 pounds on it and there wasn't an ounce of fat on him.

→-←

On May 15, the day before the opening of qualifications, forty-three cars went through tune-ups. The 50-year-old Chet Miller, holder of the track record, was clocked in a Novi at 138.5 mph in one lap. He kept going and tried for more. The temperamental Novi got away from him coming out of the first turn and Miller crashed thunderously into the upper wall. He died instantly amid a crumpled tangle of metal. Duke Nalon, his stable-mate in the other Novi; Jean Marcenac, the cars' chief mechanic; and Wilbur Shaw, Speedway president and three-time winner, wept openly.

Vukovich was quiet. Miller had been one of his favorites. Whatever it is other drivers feel when one of their number is killed, Bill kept to himself.

The first qualification day inherited still more rain. The Keck garage was full once more, this time including Agajanian and Bettenhausen, who this year was driving for the colorful, cordial Aggie. Agajanian, scanning the wall, eyed Vukovich's qualifying times in '52, and couldn't resist a jibe. "Hell, Vuky, you went down from a 139 to 137. What was the matter? Scared?"

Bill gave it back: "Here I give you guys sixty grand and you insult me."

The garage was in good spirits, in its brightest mood of the month. The Keck Kids were ready, and it was qualifying time at last.

The rain threatened to stay all day, but the hour had finally presented itself when they could start squaring the account. The talk naturally was of speeds and soon someone jokingly suggested to Vukovich that he "shut off at the gate." At the Speedway there is a crossover gate at the end of the main straightaway, at the very mouth of the southwest first turn. A Speedway driver's nerve is measured by how near he comes to the gate before he takes his foot off the throttle in deference to the curve now suddenly confronting him. Members of the race profession and of the press and radio stand at the pit walls and listen for the back-off of the engine and make note of the shut-off spot. The engine back-off reveals to onlookers each driver's point, but Vukovich's was one of the deepest carries. But for his needlers he had only: "The hell with you. I'm not shutting off at the gate. I'm too scared to."

"I'll bet somebody does a 140," Bettenhausen said.

"I know that," Bill replied.

"Who?" Agajanian asked, looking directly at Vukovich.

Bill refused to rise to the bait. "The one guy who could do it isn't here now," he said.

He meant Chet Miller. He said it in a flat, casual tone. No one mentioned a name.

In strode retired Mauri Rose, an old pro, three-time victor. He was greeted admiringly. Soon he had the floor, sitting on his haunches, for all chairs had long since been occupied. Everyone else became silent. Vukovich, normally a conversation leader, grew especially attentive, as did Bettenhausen.

Rose, sporting a mustache and smoking a pipe, had been brittle as a competitor but was more mellow and communicative in his retirement. He opened with a grin and declared, in his deliberate way:

"'A guy just paid me a compliment. He says, 'You know, Mauri, I've been watching a guy go into the turns who reminds me of you …Vukovich.' You know, I feel complimented because (and he looked at Vukovich now for the first time) you've been going!" Bill grinned, embarrassed, and Bettenhausen smiled.

Rose continued: "You know, you gotta have luck in this business. I've been lucky. Shaw disagrees with me. He says you don't have to be lucky; but he does agree with me that you can't afford to be unlucky … which is the same thing, the negative. Of course, you have to work hard all right. But you have to have the breaks. I had the breaks. As far as drivers go, there were a lot of drivers better than I. Rex Mays finished second to me in '41, but he was a better driver than I. Of course, Rex was a little hard on an engine. You can race around here a lot of years and not win.

"You know, Vuky, one year something will go wrong with the steering mechanism, and the next year something else falls off and the next something else until you go all the way around the car before you win." He grinned and so did everyone else.

Vukovich spoke now for the first time, thoughtfully, agreeably.

"That's right. I was trying to make up my mind whether to come in or not with that steering … and I throttled down once and then back up and I throttled down again. That damned wheel wouldn't turn more than that (he made a small radius with his hands) and I ran into the damned wall and got out and walked away."

For the first time since his return to the Indianapolis Speedway, Bill Vukovich appeared to have forgiven the fates. He had been lucky to escape injury.

Rose went on: "It's the breaks … a quarter-of-a-mile up the track a guy spins and a lap later someone loops and you've won the race. I had begun to feel uneasy in a car, so I decided that was enough for me. In those last years a guy would needle me about not driving so hard. Duke (Nalon) always did. So, I'd say to the guy, 'OK, so I'm old and yellow;

so, what are you going to do about it?' And the guy says, 'I gotta be somewhere.' And he leaves.

"It takes a combination to win this, Vuky. As far as you're concerned, you should win. You have the car and the mechanics; all you need is the luck. You learn a little from everyone here. When I was driving for Keck that was the first harmonious crew I was ever with. It takes all that."

❧

Rain continued to fall into the next morning, the second trials date, and nerve ends were becoming exposed. It was obvious Vukovich had not completely compromised with the fates. He was a taut bundle again, short on conversation with all but his crew, shutting out everything and everybody while pacing restlessly. When the weather let up at noon the crew moved the car into the qualification line at the apron, second to go out. There was the vital pole position to be won, the $1,000 that went with it, a possible additional $1,000 for the swiftest time ultimately in the field, and the obvious advantage of being in the first row on race day.

Vukovich was called away by a long-distance phone call at the Thompsons and had to deal with heavy traffic, both motorized and pedestrian, each direction. He accepted a ride to the Thompson home but walked back to save time. He was in his seat in the pits before the weather cleared enough for qualifications to begin around 2:20 p.m.

He wore a blue racing suit, new bowling shoes, chamois-skin gloves, the scarred helmet, and clean, wide Polaroid goggles. For the officials who walked up to wish him luck and re-brief him on procedure he had only a perfunctory handwave. He nodded to his crew — and was off. A slight rain began to fall.

Bill took the green flag immediately, knowing the rain wouldn't hold off long enough for the luxury of a warm-up lap or two. His first lap speed: 139.147. There was applause. Then, 138.568. Then, 138.739.

He had just flared out of the final turn of his final lap when the big, black clouds hanging over the track suddenly let go. Not a man among the 50,000 spectators — Walter Mittys all — wanted to be in his shoes as he headed his blue bolt into the home straightaway amid huge, pelting drops of rain. Every passenger car driver who had ever skidded on a wet street knew Vukovich was flirting with disaster coming down the chute.

He stayed on it, not lifting his foot until reaching the finish line. The abrupt change in speed caused the car to jump sideways, but he managed to get it pointed straight again and keep it on the track.

When he returned to his pit only his thankful crew, Agajanian, photographers, and three guards holding a now-unnecessary restraining rope awaited him in the drenching downpour. He was just as grim as while awaiting his turn, and he said over the loudspeaker that his car jumped a little in the rain but that it didn't matter. He shouted, "Gee!" when he saw the opening 139 lap and the two succeeding 138s, but he couldn't comply when Aggie jokingly told him to relax and smile.

"Let's get this pig out of here; I'm wet," he said. He then drove into his garage and began to unwrap his bundle of nerves, letting his colorful profanity flow.

Everyone peeled off soaked shirts and trousers and talked the tension away, and the nervy man who had probably just won the pole position for the 1953 500-Mile Race with a speed of 138.392 began explaining:

"Boy, I was all over the track ... no one has to tell me those bricks are slippery when they're wet ... geez, am I glad we ever qualified ... boy, when you slide a foot, it feels like a yard ... I came sideways down the straightaway in the second lap."

Having toweled himself dry, Bill put on his sports shirt. After a moment's pause, he looked down at it and noticed something was wrong. "Hell, I'm not excited," he said, sarcastically.

The shirt was on inside-out.

Travers shook his head. "I've been in bombings on the island, but that's the worst sweats I've ever had."

Coon mostly just grinned and gently wiped dry their iron-and-gasoline offspring. The others in the crew — Stu Hilborn, Jim Nairn, Mel Straw and Bill Hook — listened to Bill unwind and smiled at his expletives. Someone suggested he sit down. He responded in a burst of rare confession: "Hell, I don't want to sit down; I'm so damned excited."

His thoughts jumped. "Where's that damned Aggie?" he said with an impish leer. "Tell him we can qualify faster in the rain than he can on a dry track."

Next, he spotted last year's qualifying speeds on the wall and said, "Geez, we were faster than last year."

Travers: "Hell, we worked all year."

Vukovich, reaching for the needle: "Yeh, we get one-fourth-mile-an-hour faster in a year."

Coon: "That Keck says, 'Boy, the speed comes hard, doesn't it?'"

And then Travers, out of sheer joy and addressing Bill by the crew's pet nickname for him, simply shouted: "Hey, Smoky!" There were beatific smiles all around.

Bill then turned his attention back to the car. "That turtle still doesn't feel like it's going. The only time it sounded good was when it went sideways."

Bill was beginning to relax now and when Freddie Agabashian stopped at the door to offer his congratulations, he replied: "Boy, I just took my foot off (he raised his right leg) and kept it off the rest of the time."

And as it does in all the best fiction, the sun suddenly broke through as they all went out to relax over a cup of coffee.

⤜⤛

Eventually, seven qualified on the day — Agabashian next to Bill at 137.546, and McGrath third, at 136.602, to complete the first row.

Later, Travers and Coon elaborated on the qualification run.

"We had an understanding when he was out there, he would decide about keeping going," Coon said. "He's that kind of guy. He knows what's going on." Travers added: "He's a champion. We were sick about last year, but the reprieve comes when you know everyone came out alive ... There was just something about him when we first saw him ... The smartest thing we ever did was to hire him ... He may insult you, but there's something about him you like."

So, for the next twelve days Vukovich was comparatively calm as half-a-hundred other entries sweated out the search for additional speed in practice and then fought for a place in the starting field the following weekend of qualifying.

He was the primary conversation piece now at the track and in the newspapers; he had become a public figure. But nobody knew much about him except what he had done in a race car, and it wasn't going to be easy to get to know him. The spotlight made him uncomfortable, and he answered questions from strangers with short words and sentences before quickly walking away.

Ed Elisian was one of the few who knew him. He was a recipient of the Vukovich largess, bestowed with Vukovich gruffness. They had met in California the previous year when Elisian, wanting to graduate from midgets to the big cars, was seeking a ride to Indianapolis. Bill was walking across a racetrack and Ed stopped him. They talked of Indianapolis and Bill said he was driving back alone and invited Ed to join him. Okay. They talked of midget driving and Ed mentioned that he had gone around a guy on the outside in an indoor race in Oakland, the only man to do it except for Vukovich. Bill, who had been present that day, answered: "Yeh, I know, but I was the first guy to do it."

Vukovich called Elisian worthless, lazy, good-for-nothing, used him to let off steam — but, despite hardly knowing him, let him have his midget to drive.

"Vuky is the finest guy you'd want to know," Elisian said. "Back home he's as friendly as he can be; he's a wonderful family man. He's more devoted to his wife and kids than ninety percent of these other guys. But something happens to Vuky when he comes to Indianapolis. He knows he's going to race and get out in front and all those other guys are going to chase him. And he gets gripey and crabs at people and bitches. He's on edge. He has to let off steam.

"He doesn't expound his virtues. Win, lose or draw he's the same guy. Everybody has to live on a certain social level; Vuky doesn't try to put on airs. On a racetrack he's either going to spin out, hit the wall, or win; no fourth or fifth place for him … In '48 when he was going so good in the midgets and won all that money his wife told me he had $4,000 lent out — and without collateral or anything — and you know that's an awful lot of money to be lending. He never worked a deal on anyone. He's always been independent, had his own money. He could probably stick around here and get himself a really good deal, but he doesn't polish any apples and he doesn't speak well; he just wants to come out here and race — and blow off all the other guys.

"He always needles everybody, but you know where you stand with him. He doesn't needle you unless he likes you … I tell him about guys (race drivers) making money speaking and his says, 'Balls, while they're speaking my Drake was making $35,000.'"

Meanwhile, Vukovich worried his foes. Andy Granatelli, owner of the car qualified by Agabashian that would start next to Bill, admitted he didn't know what to do about strategy for the race. One day, standing at the pit wall with him, two newspapermen asked Andy about his plans for race day, especially in combating Vukovich.

"What would you do?" Granatelli asked. "Would you race Vuky? You know he's going to charge out there. Would you let some of the guys go all out, like they have done the last few years and get a lap or so on you and not blow up and beat you? We could set a pace, have Freddie go 131 or 133, which he could do all day, and let the other guys blow up.

"As far as I'm concerned Vuky won last year's race. Everybody feels the same way. He went out and got it. We weren't worrying about Ruttman, we were worried about Vuky. Ruttman came in last year with pistons melted. Vuky is the drivingest sonuvabitch that ever came out here. He'll punish hell out of a car, but we know it'll go 500 miles. We've got to set up our gear ratio and plan our race and we've got to decide what we want to do, what'll win. Should we race Vuky? Should we try to go ahead of him or stay in the same lap? Or lay back and hope he'll blow up? Do we know Freddie can drive 500 miles all out? Does Freddie know? Does anybody know?"

Over in the Belanger garage, Frenchy Sirois, mechanic, brought up Bill's name. "That Vukovich is a race man's race driver. He comes into the garage and I says, 'Vuky, what are you doing around here; you're qualified and got nothing to worry about.' He says, 'You know, Frenchy, this place is like a magnet; I can't stay away.' Boy, if he jumps out there in front — and you know he isn't going to let those $150s (the lap prize had been boosted to $150 a lap) go without a struggle, he'll have a helluva lead built up by the first pit stop."

This was what Bill Vukovich had done to the 500-Mile Race. The speculation was constant. What about the first lap? Would Vukovich try to make it first into the turn? Agabashian's car was a great accelerator. McGrath liked to race. Bill himself once said, "If some other guy beats me there why should I try to get in there? There's 500 miles to go. I can catch him the sixth or seventh lap."

Those who knew Vukovich didn't believe that any more than he did.

The field of thirty-three eventually filled, leaving fifty entries out. Nearly all those fallen fifty had started with at least a $25,000 investment in the car, and for them, at the end of nearly a month of expenses, sweat had turned to tears, anxiety had become frustration, hope had become despair. Along the way one man had been killed, two hospitalized, one with critical burns, and there had been numerous other accidents, including three spins by George Connor, veteran of fourteen 500-Mile Races. He interpreted the third spin as a cue and decided to sit this race out. Both Ruttman and Wallard were missing. Troy had been injured, Lee burned, each after his triumph, to perpetuate the jinx that seemed to be following recent "500"winners.

It was the fastest field in history, with a remarkable qualifying average of 136.435 mph. Vukovich's speed of 138.392 had held up under the onslaught. Second to him in pace was Bill Holland, 1949 winner, in a surprising comeback at 137.868, and third was Johnnie Parsons, at 137.667.

Vukovich, who had been at ease for more than a week, began to simmer again as race day approached. Once, coming out of deep thought, without provocation, he blurted out: "Boy, I came back here this year ready to go 140. I'm still mad ... those butchers."

He'd slandered the mechanics again. He wasn't serious about the name-calling; he was about the speed. He was becoming a little more nervous, a little less likely to sit still. Soon his ribbing began to diminish and his observations about the car became sincere.

➤◄

Three days before the race the car was stripped down. Coon spent five hours checking camshafts. He looked for an oil leak in the engine, which Travers didn't believe existed. Travers was trying to reshape a part of the frame, alternately banging away with a gavel and softening the spot with a blow torch, while Nairn and Straw swabbed the outside of the frame with wet cloths to keep the heat from radiating.

In a corner, on the workbench, stood a signboard, to be used in the race. In block letters of red phosphorescent paint, it read, "Go 140." An arrow pointed to the right. Was this to be the Kecks' goal? Or just a psychological scare to throw at the opposition?

Mechanic Herb Porter, who was to join them for the race, had given the Kecks the board. The crew had wanted to surprise Bill with it, but he spotted it. So, the sign was formally introduced along with a three-layer cake for Bill, but there was little levity about the speed; 140 mph with or without thirty-two other cars on the track prompted only serious contemplation.

Coon found the oil leak after a final pre-race shakedown, and decided to use a rubber hose in the line rather than metal because vibration wouldn't affect it as much. Bill noticed something on the engine he didn't like and suggested attaching a safety spring. Travers and Coon agreed. Keck, who had flown in for the race, stayed in the background in the garage, rarely speaking. Once Bill let out a ringing shout, "To the gate!" as if it was time to race. It wasn't, but it reflected his anxiety over the challenge ahead.

The crew practiced pit stops feverishly for two hours under "game conditions," with Bill rolling in as he would during the race. Other crews, some derisively, wondered why. The Kecks decided they would change all four tires in each stop, rather than only those that needed changed, so that each stop would be identical and each man would have the same task. They adopted Jim Nairn's idea that one man would first make a circuit of the car, loosening the hub wing nuts to dismount the tires, then make another circuit tightening them. Nairn was selected. Bill's cue for applying the brakes would be Porter dropping the head of a hammer.

Vukovich, the polesitter, shakes hands with Freddie Agabashian at the drivers' meeting before the 1953 "500." Jack McGrath, who started third, is next to Agabashian. (Bob Gates collection)

In those tight hours before the race Sam Hanks, who was in the third row, could be heard on a phone: "It's mental fatigue that begins to get you at 350 miles. There's no training you can do for the race, except just to drive all the time. None of the guys take gym exercise, because you don't work the muscles you'll need driving. Some of the boys have had their legs tie up along about 300 miles. I just drive for the training I need for my arms and shoulders and hands."

Vukovich, meanwhile, continued his bedside pushups and spent five minutes daily on the steering wheel machine until its shocks wore out. He stopped the trips to a chiropractor he had made a couple of times. He felt pretty good, so he didn't want to risk, as he said, having a chiropractor "twist something and give me a kink for the race."

He always appeared to be busy, walking, walking, head down, with an absorbed expression. In repose, his dark brow presented a picture of weighty concentration. Mostly he let the crew alone while he worked off some of his nervous energy fiddling with his midget race car, which he was going to let someone drive at the race across the street from the Speedway the night before the "500."

He continued to be impatient with publicity and with newspaper and radio reporters. He would swear when asked to meet with someone and while he might comply, he wouldn't go out of his way. His typical response was, "Damn! Always bothering you!" He made two dinner dates with me and failed to keep both. He was too preoccupied and unwilling to comply with anything that restricted his schedule, no matter how brief or undemanding.

The day before the race scores of pictures were taken at the drivers' meeting with the actress hired to kiss the winner — it was Jane Greer this time — and front row starters Agabashian and McGrath. Vukovich, the polesitter, was noticeable again by his absence.

The Indianapolis News souvenir edition form chart picked the personable and colorful Parsons in the Belond Equa-Flow to win at the short odds of 6-1, concluding: "Car is cracking new offset beauty in hands of victory-hungry former winner who is at his best in Speedway traffic. This one gets the shaky nod." It selected Vukovich next at 7-1, explaining: "Almost everyone picks this one to win, which imposes heavy handicap at the start. Great driver, great car. Should have won last year. Will be looking out for scads of lap prizes."

Members of the Champion 100-Mile-an-Hour Club were split in their feelings between the likeable, cooperative Agabashian and Vukovich. Ruttman chose Vukovich. "He's a lot smarter than people give him credit for being."

The average fan, not caring that Bill didn't court him and recognizing Bill's single-mindedness about racing and winning, picked Vukovich.

6

"I should have stuffed some ears in my cotton."

Revenge Served Hot

Race day unfolded under a blue sky, with a multitude that was to reach 175,000 filing into the grounds. But there was a difference. It was going to be extremely hot this year, with high humidity and gusts of wind reaching 25 mph.

At 9:40, 1 hour and 20 minutes before the start of the race, Vukovich sat relaxed in the garage with Keck and the crew. He wasn't as nervous as he had been during the waiting period. Race day brought relief, the moment he'd been sweating out.

Duane Carter, starting in the ninth row, stuck his head in to wish Bill luck: "After you come in first, save a little for ole Carter, Vuky," he said. Bill smiled widely and answered softly and deliberately, for he was being drawn from a deep introspection. "When you go by, hook onto me, Duane, and take me with you."

A few minutes later he was in a corner tying his shirt tails with small strings to his undershorts to keep the shirt from billowing. He put in his pocket the silver dollar Fred Gerhardt had given him for good luck before he left Fresno, which he had accepted as a friend despite his rejection of superstitions.

At 10:20 the first cars were pushed out to the starting line, a thrill in itself — a slowly-moving file of shining, spotless machines packing power and destruction, rolled by neat crews in brightly-colored uniforms.

Ominously, one of the members of the color guard of the Purdue University marching band fainted from the heat during the pre-race ceremony. Soon, two drum majorettes fell victim, too.

At 10:40, during the national anthem, Vukovich stood and stared at the steering bars on the right side of the car, where his troubles had been last year. The last note fading, he checked his goggles — and a dozen cameras focused on him.

Several cockpits had been covered to ward off the sun until the drivers stepped into them. There was a flurry of turmoil as contestants, officials, and crews wished each other luck. Vukovich sat on a tire, taking good wishes perfunctorily, his face locked in determination. He wore a gray sports shirt, khaki pants, pith helmet, and black bowling shoes.

At 10:55 — only five minutes left — Jack Beckley, McGrath's mechanic, noted the rising temperature: "It's going to be the survival of the fittest." Travers was impatient: "Let's get this show on the road; it's time for deeds."

To ease the pressure in this last contact with his crew, he conducted a lighthearted rundown: "Got grease in the transmission? Air in the tires? Check the oil?" And then, apropos of nothing, he said: "I never felt better and had less."

The two-minute bomb went off. Galvanized, Bill Vukovich, who had a score to settle, quickly tugged at his gloves, stepped into the car and adjusted his helmet. His face had a gray cast. His expression, behind goggles, was uncompromising, his mouth a hard, thin line. No grimmer determination ever wrote itself across a man's face. The meld that came from rugged ancestry, adverse environment, disappointment, pride and confidence blended into an arresting countenance.

A multi-thousand-throated murmur rose to a roar as the pace car pulled away and the thirty-three drivers jockeyed into their qualifying positions, three abreast along eleven rows, for the flying start when they completed the circuit.

They completed the warmup lap amid a cloud of dust and the thunder of spine-tingling shouts from the fans. Once the field reached the starting line on the main straightaway, Vukovich suddenly shot out and took a stunning half a block lead into the first turn.

The record for a first lap, which is hampered by the pace car's speed and heavy traffic, was 126.564 mph, set by Nalon in a Novi in 1949. On a track where advances in speed normally come in thousandths of a second, Vukovich whirled around his initial lap in 133.097. He was chasing his destiny.

Later, when asked what he thought when he saw the great and growing gap he'd opened, Bill would say, "I jammed my foot on the damned throttle, dove it into the turn, and looked back — and the sonuvabitches didn't want to race!"

Actually, they tried. Manny Ayulo took up the first chase but after three laps Vukovich was still 100 yards in front. Agabashian next moved into the challenger's spot, with Art Cross, Ayulo, and Parsons following in order, but Bill still moved away. Suddenly on the fourth lap Andy Linden spun and wrecked. He was unhurt but out of the race. The caution light was lit while his car was removed.

Caution lights are a handicap for the leader. Drivers can't improve their position while running at a slower speed, but they often get away with closing the gap on the car ahead of them. This light lasted fifty-five seconds.

Vukovich stayed in front when the green light flashed, and the trailers juggled for position behind him. The Keck crew sent Bill messages on their new board. On the thirty-first lap he was shown a "6S," with the arrow pointing to the left, to tell him he was six seconds ahead of the second car. Occasionally he was shown "P1" to reaffirm he was in first place.

He nodded calmly to every sign while traveling 175 mph down the home stretch. Once he responded to Hilborn's message with a thumb-and-forefinger circle meaning *Everything's OK.*

The excessive heat was scorching tires, and pit stops began startlingly early. Cross stopped. Then, abruptly, Vukovich did as well on Lap 49. So did Ayulo, leaving Agabashian in the lead.

Beautifully efficient tire changes and refueling got Bill out in forty-seven seconds — the "game-condition" rehearsals paying off. While his crew labored frantically, he accepted a paper cupful of water from Keck, who leaned over the pit wall. Keck offered a clean pair of goggles, but Bill refused them.

Now he had to regain the lead.

It took him just five laps. He got a "P1" on the crew's message board, then an "OK." As he reached his sixty-sixth lap the race began to settle into a smooth rhythm. The hectic maneuvering abated after the initial pit stops and now the other drivers shared a challenge — catch the unrelenting Vukovich.

The weather presented a challenge all its own, however. The Firestone people, who had been feeding an abnormal number of tires to the crews, checked the track temperature. It read 130 degrees. For the fans in the stands and the infield it was 93 with oppressive humidity.

Soon there was a flurry in the pits. Carl Scarborough, having just completed his seventieth lap, got out of his car and stepped over the wall while his crew worked frantically. He needed a relief driver. Then, suddenly, he collapsed in his chair from the heat and carbon monoxide gas resulting from a fire that had been quickly extinguished. His crew stretched him out on the concrete and yelled for an ambulance. Scarborough, appearing gray, was lifted in as photographers flocked around, snapping hurriedly. A burly mechanic shook his fist at them and ordered them to stop. They didn't. The ambulance sped away to the infield hospital. The race was less than an hour-and-a-half old.

Vukovich, meanwhile, still led, still set a record pace, still clicked off $150 per lap.

The Speedway breaks down its records into twenty-three segments — the first, second, fourth, and tenth laps and every ten laps thereafter. By the eightieth lap Vukovich had established new marks for all but the one at seventy laps, set by Ruttman in '52. Two yellow lights had slowed him momentarily, but by the eightieth lap he had boosted his average to 131.346, bettering the standard of 130.832 by Ruttman the previous year.

Bill soon lost one of his closer competitors when Parsons' crew noticed an oil leak while he was in the pits. Then, even more surprisingly, Parsons collapsed and was rushed to the hospital. One of the hardier drivers, Parsons' normal procedure during pit stops was to hop out of the car and do a bear dance to improve his circulation. But in these conditions, he couldn't even stand up.

"I put three cushions under the seat so I could sit higher and get some air across my shoulders and neck," Parsons explained later. "My uniform was so oil-soaked I couldn't get any air in. I had unbuttoned my uniform, but it didn't help."

The heat also claimed Jerry Hoyt, a healthy 21-year-old. He was relieved by husky Chuck Stevenson. Then Agabashian, slight, wiry, and durable, signaled for relief — thus answering Granatelli's question at least for this day. When Freddie had pulled himself together again, he said, "I knew I wasn't right when I began doing things I wouldn't normally do. I was getting sloppy, out of the groove … I could feel my heart pounding so heavily I looked down at my chest expecting to see it. The race is like driving in a furnace. When you try to catch your breath and your lungs feel like they're on fire, then you've had it."

The driver substitutions were coming quickly now. Jim Rathmann, in the low-slung Travelon Special, emerged from it wrung out and bitter: "I just got so damned sick in that damned pig I couldn't take it." Eddie Johnson took over and later described the conditions as "hotter than 700 hells." Linden tried Hoyt's car, the Zink Special, after Stevenson had succumbed to the heat. Andy was the third to try it but gave up as well. The car was still in running order, but nobody wanted in.

Bettenhausen asked for help, totally exhausted after 113 laps. He was too weak to remove his crash helmet and his crew helped him to the pit wall, where he gulped huge quantities of water. Hanks had to be assisted to a shady spot, where his crew fanned him and ran water to him. All this was going on with the race a little past the midway point. Nalon kept racing, but he made frequent pit stops merely to have another bucketful of water dumped on him.

Cockpits of the low-slung roadsters were proving inadequately ventilated for this brutal day, and fumes from fuel exhaust and nitromethane, a fuel stimulant, aggravated the effects of the heat.

Beckley had said it — this was survival of the fittest. And where was Vukovich on this pitiless, oven-temperature day, the hottest in all Speedway history? He was clicking off the laps like a taxi meter, oblivious to the conditions, leading so convincingly that the focus shifted to the fight for second place and to the frantic pit activity. His lead was nearly

Vukovich reaches for a cup of water during a pit stop on the 172nd lap while his crew hustles to change four tires and refuel. Many drivers needed relief because of the oppressive heat, but he went the distance. (Bob Gates collection)

two laps, so he absorbed a second pit stop of sixty-one seconds without losing the lead. He passed cars wherever he came on them, going under or around, and uncannily avoided the sideways jumps and spins that posed trouble.

In the stands, Esther kept swallowing nerve pills.

He was setting records — for speed, for lap prize money in a single race, for total lap prize money earned by a driver in a career — and this was only his third Indianapolis 500. He was achieving a level of public recognition perhaps never before reached by a Speedway competitor.

Bill deferred to the heat that was destroying others only to the extent of tucking his left heel underneath him when he could, to keep it from roasting near the oil line.

He came in on Lap 172 for his third pit stop. He was two laps ahead of the eager Cross and three ahead of Paul Russo, in Agabashian's car. While his crew scurried to get him out in forty-nine seconds — another remarkably fast refueling and change of four tires that brought loud cheers from the grandstands — he sat composed, poured water down his back, drank a cupful, and yelled into Travers' ear: "Don't fill the tank too full because it wants to throw the front end!"

Standing unobtrusively at the rear of the pit area, unnoticeable to Bill, was an old hand, Henry Banks, with a helmet and goggles in his hand. The Kecks, aware that so many men were succumbing to the heat, had asked Banks to stand by for Bill's stop in the event Bill, too, might need relief.

One glance reassured them; he could go the distance.

Now the entourage to the Bullpen began for Jane Greer and her court. Esther, however, remained in her seat. She remembered last year. So did the crowd, which now crossed fingers for Bill. He remembered, too. With only a few laps to go, he prayed a little.

He stayed in character, though, and passed Nalon in a turn, as if he were trailing in the race instead of leading it.

The joyful preparations for Bill's victory were interrupted, however, by a news bulletin that first reached the pit area and then went crackling like an electric current through the grounds. Scarborough was dead. For ninety minutes, medical personnel in the infield hospital had given him artificial respiration and oxygen, and then, in desperation, had cut open his chest and massaged his heart. All had failed. Carl Scarborough, age 38, father of three, became the twenty-fourth driver to die at the Indianapolis Motor Speedway.

Vukovich appeared tense as he turned into the 200th lap. The fans began standing, craning to watch him every foot of the way. The 100,000 within range of the home stretch strained to see if he appeared once more out of the last turn. He did and raced toward the waving checkered flag to thunderous applause as he squared his record with fate.

He had completely dominated the most grueling 500-Mile Race in history, a four-hour battle in which only fourteen of the original thirty-three cars were still running at the end ... in which only five drivers went the distance without relief ... in which a record fifteen driver substitutions were made, along with a record ninety-one pit stops and a

Mechanic Frank Coon, left, was a key member of the braintrust that put Vukovich and the rest of the Keck Kids "on Broadway." (IMS Photos)

record 206 tire changes. There had been five accidents, one death, fifteen drivers taken to the hospital from heat exhaustion.

He had traveled at record speed along the way, although 9 minutes, 28 seconds of running under the yellow caution light had protected the record average for the full 500 miles. He had led 195 of the 200 laps for a record $29,250 in lap money, part of a record winner's purse that would be presented the following evening.

He was greeted in Victory Bullpen by clicking cameras, noisy newsreel photographers, jabbering radio broadcasters and insistent newspaper reporters, along with track officials and eager commercial representatives shoving their way to the front. His faithful crew and generous boss awaited him but were forced to the background by the crush. He was the grimmest winner in years, his face a heavy layer of oil and dirt that couldn't hide his deep fatigue. He drove far into the wire

"The grimmest winner in years," Vukovich is kissed by his wife, Esther (left) and actress Jane Greer in the Victory Bullpen. (IMS Photos)

enclosure and started fumbling, ineptly, with his gloves. Goggles came off next, then helmet — and he still hadn't said anything.

Esther was among those waiting. In contrast to the escort of eight policemen given the Hollywood actress, she had been forced to climb the Bullpen fence and identify herself to get in.

It took nearly four minutes until Bill realized people were talking to him. He could only respond with "How's that?" And then: "I can't hear a damned thing!"

He was half-angry, still pent up. The roar of the race had deafened him. He looked stunned, staggered more by this reception than the race he had won. He stood up, but immediately sat down. "It's hot!" he said.

He eagerly took the cold water offered him and a Coke. He kissed Esther, then, dutifully, Jane Greer, and when his questioners demanded he say something he repeated time and again that it was "hotternhell."

"Which was the toughest, the heat or the competition?"

"Heat." He showed a burned left hand. "It was a hot son-of-a-bitch."

He put a wet cloth on the back of his neck.

"Say something!" the microphone men pleaded.

"It was a good, hot race is about all I can say."

"What are you going to do with the money, buy a racer?"

"Hell, no!"

Quickly leaving his wife and crew, he bolted the enclosure and fought his way on foot through the pressing mob to his garage. He had not connected with his crew in the Bullpen amid the stampede of officials seeking his attention and was eager to see them.

Soon he was slumped in a beach chair as the crew and other friends, now caught up, held back the hero-worshippers.

"I've never been so tired in my life."

His eyes, normally bright, were lifeless as he stared at the floor, a wet wash towel perched on his matted hair, face as grimy as his shirt and khakis. He took off his shoes and rolled his socks down to his toes to cool his feet.

Well-wishers who managed to get past the restraining rope wasted their compliments. He could hardly lift his eyes to greet them, and he couldn't hear. Esther sat next to him, receiving for him. Once she

Vukovich acknowledges the fans from the Victory Bullpen while Speedway president Wilbur Shaw, with binoculars, looks on. (IMS Photos)

Sweat-soaked and oil-stained, he had helping hands while returning to his garage. (IMS Photos)

remarked: "All I need here are my kids." Bill's brother Mike stood happily in the background.

In a bit, Travers, seeking a return to normal atmosphere, began to needle: "Hey, Vuky, you're supposed to win 'em all. You lost two." (At the time, the crew thought Bill had led all but two laps; an official check later had him out of the lead for five.) Travers went on: "Everything was just the way we planned. No trouble. Nobody panicked."

Howard Keck, who owned the operation but was allergic to attention and crowds, was nowhere in sight. He preferred to stay away until the hub bub expired.

One handshaker, with ill-considered timing, asked Bill, "Did you hear about Carl?"

Esther cut in, sharply: "Don't tell him anything."

It was too late. The man tried to stop himself, couldn't: "Scarborough died from the heat."

Bill's face went long, Esther glared, the informant made an awkward exit. He said nothing. He then rose wearily, ambled stiff and aching to the car, sat on the right front tire and began talking with the crew. The atmosphere now was of mutual admiration and affection.

"I didn't know it was so hot," he said. "The temperature gauge went out about 150 laps … I was sure praying those last laps … I should have stuffed some ears in my cotton."

Too weary to reassemble the words correctly, he let them stay that way.

He thanked the crew for the smooth pit stops that helped him increase his lead, but in his typical, inverted way: "Boy, I was in them an hour!"

"Hell, everybody was getting relief," he added. "Every time I saw a car there was a new chauffeur in it."

A man with a microphone wanted him to speak over the public address system to reach the thousands who were still on the grounds, either unwilling to leave yet or caught in the gigantic traffic jam. Bill answered dutifully, mechanically. He wanted to end it quickly:

"We want to rest a little bit before we say anything … We figured we'd lead all laps we could because you don't know how long you'll run

… I knew fellows were getting relief, but I wasn't too bad at any time … That water sure tasted good."

The interview was over.

Then, turning to his crew, he blurted out: "I don't want to talk to anybody."

Coon: "Smoky, you put us on Broadway today."

Vukovich: "I'm gonna build my own race car next year."

Travers: "It's starting again."

Hilborn, dryly: "He's feeling better."

⊷⊶

An hour later, Vukovich was still partially deaf and still having to greet people wanting to shake his hand. Travers had left the stuffy garage, whose doors were still closed, to cool off and Keck had slipped in.

Once, Bill wheeled toward the car and exclaimed, "This pig!" Then he looked up at Keck to ask in mock solicitation: "You happy, Howard?" Keck, a man of even fewer words, merely grinned at him.

The crew showed him the marvelous pit stop times but he still refused to say thanks except in his unconventional way: "I could have done that good; got out and changed 'em myself."

Agajanian, who had benefited from Vukovich's bad luck last year, arrived and shouted, "Where's that goddamn stroker!" Then he kissed him.

"I was running easy, for Crissakes," Bill said. "I'm gonna make this (race) a thousand miles."

"I figured out why you went so fast," Aggie said. "Fresno is so hot all these guys weren't used to heat like you."

He then softened his tone: "Bettenhausen says, 'We've got to take our hats off to the guy; he showed us the way around.'"

"Why didn't they hook on?"

"They figured you were going too fast for them to hook on."

Pause.

"I should have had some cotton in my ears."

"Why didn't you have any? Didn't you think you were going to finish?"

Finally, a chance to relax with Esther in his garage. "I've never been so tired in my life." (Bob Gates collection)

The doors were opened to let in some badly needed fresh air. Seeing the pressing crowd, Bill retreated to the rear of the garage.

"I don't want to talk to anybody," he said. His temporary deafness was a convenience now.

Agajanian remained serious: "Sure glad you won. You won twice and got paid for once."

McGrath walked in with his wife.

"Hello, McGrath." Bill's tone was warm.

Jack took Bill's hand in both of his. "Congratulations, boy."

Bill, somewhat uncomfortably: "If we'd had a good engine, we'd really set sail."

"We heard you went to the hospital," Lois McGrath said. "We had to come around."

"Yeah, I had a boy," Bill said.

Lois nodded toward Esther and said, "We wanted to take her down (to the Bullpen) with twenty laps to go but she said, 'Nothing doing.'"

Then I stepped forward and said quietly, "I'm proud of you, Bill."

He leaned in and answered quickly, in a low, intimate tone: "You have to be lucky to win this damned thing!"

He said it not with false modesty, for he had none, but with a trace of irritation. Irritated, because the sheer force of his will was not enough, as he knew from last year's misfortune.

But Bill Vukovich had his revenge.

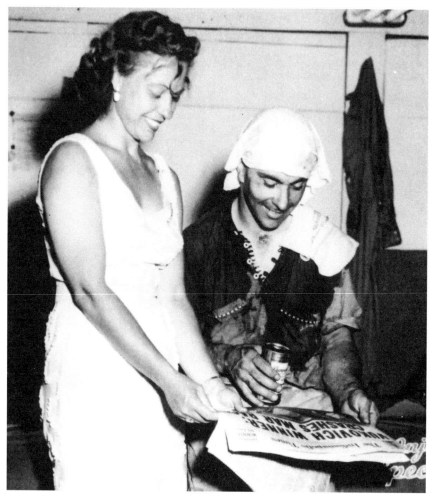

Bill and Esther admire The Indianapolis Times *coverage in the immediate aftermath of the race. The local newspapers rushed out editions as soon as the race ended, flying them to the track by helicopter.* (Bob Gates collection)

7

"Everybody wants to wine and dine you.
That's lovely, but a lot of crap."

The Spoils of Victory

At the Victory Dinner the following night, in the honor spot at the head table, Vukovich sat thoughtful and unsmiling through the evening's quips as Wilbur Shaw, master of ceremonies, called up each driver to the rostrum in the inverse order of finish. Bill wore a cardigan sports jacket with white shirt and tie, his closest concession to a suit. He took off the jacket for a while because of the heat in the banquet hall, as did others, and smoked a cigar.

When Paul Russo collected his prize, he remarked, "We'll be back again and do all right if there aren't too many Vukoviches." Nalon said, "We'll be back next year to give that Vukovich another go." When Shaw introduced Jim Rathmann, who had led for one lap, Rathmann remarked, "Anytime this Vuky is out there it's a man's job to get even one lap from him."

Bill stared soberly at the ceiling throughout the evening, as if he hadn't heard. Then it came his turn, and as Shaw announced that Bill had won the fattest total of money in Speedway history — $89,496.96 — Bill stepped shyly up to the microphone and the hall rose in an ovation. He managed timid half-smiles for the photographers. When it was time for him to speak, he murmured in an embarrassed monotone: "Well, about all I can say is, when you drive for Howard Keck and his guys, you're in for a good ride." And he sat down.

Vukovich, meeting at the microphone with three-time winner Wilbur Shaw at the Victory Dinner, did not care for public formalities. (IMS Photos)

Posing with his fellow front row starters Jack McGrath (left) and Freddie Agabashian was less stressful. (IMS Photos)

There was a collective gasp from the disappointed listeners, who had looked forward to an expansive recitation that always had come from the exuberant winner.

Afterwards, in the comfortable company of his crew and close friends, and away from the autograph hunters, he pointed a fistful of telegrams at them.

"Guess what my kids wished me," he said. "'Dear Dad, send new money. Old money gone.'" Actually, the telegram had read: "Congratulations, Daddy — Marlene and Billy." He jabbed Travers and Coon about having put them on Broadway, stuck the telegrams and his trophy in a suitcase that was part of his winnings and accused Travers and Coon of trying to take it. With fake dissatisfaction he complained, "The payoff wasn't big enough; shoulda got $100,000."

The lush world of endorsement revenue was now open if he wanted to live in it. He could luxuriate for a year, selling his name and his triumph. There was an easy $500 in appearance money that promoters at scores of the smaller tracks throughout the country would gladly offer and even increase if he would come a few days early and help publicize the race.

"Race a few laps, Bill," or, "Say a few words, Bill; we'll send you a check."

He hadn't yet caught his breath when he was hustled by plane the next morning to New York to appear that night on Firestone's national television program to lend his endorsement of their tires. Host Wilbur Shaw tried to prod him into telling a little of himself and the race. Miserable under makeup and the hot lights and the fawning attention, Bill managed only to say in low, barely audible tones:

"I'm glad to be here."

"Well, I went about 175 miles an hour, Wilbur."

"That's right, Wilbur."

"Thank you, Mr. Firestone."

Cornered in one press conference, when asked to describe the race, he said, "I just went as fast as I could 'til I came to a corner and then I turned left." The big city reporters also wanted to know how the wife felt, and Esther replied, "You just keep gobbling nerve tablets, tighten yourself up inside and pray. When we married, I thought auto racing was glamorous. Later I found out how dangerous it was, as friend after friend was killed. Certainly, I wish Bill would give it up, but I wouldn't ask Bill to give it up for anything."

She recalled 1952: "You don't realize what a horrible experience it is when the yellow caution light goes up and the public address system announces it's your husband's car in a wreck."

Later, Travers directed the taxi driver to go to any place on Broadway. When they arrived, Jim turned to Bill and said, "See? I told you we'd put you on Broadway."

Bill countered: "Hell, I put you guys on Broadway. You were eating hamburger when I found you. Now you're eating steak."

Three days later, the crew was together again in their quiet garage at the Speedway, where Bill could unwind and reflect.

"I'm just beginning to feel good," he said. "I was kinda bushed for a couple days there. Everybody wants to wine and dine you. That's lovely, but a lot of crap. I just like to sit here with you guys and relax. I just want to go somewhere where it's shady.

"A lot of these guys just weren't in shape. I think what helped me … get out of bed, boom, boom … pushups … do about twenty or thirty. The first time you try to do ten you fall flat on your face."

The telephone kept ringing with calls from all over. Like the one from a reporter in Milwaukee for Bill, who said, "It was easy. I ate and played checkers, I had such a big lead." To the snickering audience in the garage, he twisted the left corner of his mouth in a gesture obviously meaning, *What a lot of baloney I'm handing out.*

He dug at Travers. "Christ, you hot-dog, I'm gonna get in a Novi next year and pass you tourists." Travers gave it back: "You go right ahead, and after about ten laps we'll wave to you. There were some guys around here we can get to drive for us whose tongues weren't hanging out. Cross, for one; he's hungry." Jim also stuck the last needle, offering an imitation of Bill's deadpan television appearance: "Thank you, Mr. Firestone." "About 175 miles an hour, Wilbur."

These were days to revel in now, to relax in ultimate satisfaction. Bill and Esther tarried in Indianapolis for nearly two weeks, enjoying dinner out, often with Elisian, and visiting at my home. Bill invariably beat everyone through the meal and Esther enjoyed rambling reminiscences.

Esther described the chaos in the Bullpen after Bill won: "I felt kinda lost in there. Every once in a while, Jane Greer looked at me kinda funny, wondering what to make of it … I had been standing in back and one of those fellows told me to shove in."

"I couldn't hear," Bill recalled. "I was just answering guys. You get mikes shoved into your face, everybody yakking. Some guy shoves a Coke at ya, you drink it. It doesn't taste as good as the water. It's flat. I was glad to get the hell out of there. Boy, that's the tiredest I've ever been in my life.

"Geez, the guys were really good on those pit stops," he added.

"It was a good thing he didn't come to Indianapolis until he was older; he was too wild when he was younger," Esther said.

What of the future, would he race the circuit and cash in on his reputation? "I'm getting too old for that stuff," Bill said. "It isn't worth it. I've got a good machine — best mechanics and car owner. I'll just race Indianapolis next year."

Still basking in the afterglow of victory, he jokingly told the Keck crew, and Walt Faulkner, that he planned to put a checkerboard in the cockpit next year and play checkers while he drove past the other drivers.

One night after dinner at my home while he watched Kid Gavilan and Italo Scortichini in a televised prize fight, he observed: "Why doesn't some guy fighting just go in there swinging with everything he's got — crunch, crunch — and get it over with? Why mess around and go fifteen rounds when you can get it over with? If you can't in the first round the other guy will fall down the second."

Watching the fight stirred him; he continually stood up and paced the living room and then sat down again. He made an impatient, nervous gesture, and followed it with a comment about his children or a dry remark.

The attention was beginning to get on his nerves. One day he barked impatiently: "Guys are wining and dining me and I got steak coming

Vukovich with the trophy that would soon bear his likeness. (IMS Photos)

out of my ears. If I'd finished thirty-third, I wouldn't have got a bite from anyone, isn't that right?"

The moment for Bill and Esther to return to California was approaching, but a friend from California called and said, "Vuky, I don't like to disturb you, but I believe that there is a big homecoming celebration being planned for you back home." Bill's face dropped. "I don't believe I'll go back this summer," he said.

He wasn't serious, but he did delay his return.

He submitted to the flattery of Irish Horan, who operated an automobile thrill show in Indianapolis. Horan "convinced" him that he was a celebrity and should respond so. But that night on local television, Bill, tongue-in-cheek, announced: "It doesn't take any brains to race. All race drivers just keep going 'that way.' When they come in, they don't come in for fuel and tires. Know why they come in? They stop so the brains in the pits can tell 'em what to do the second half."

He then apologized to Horan and left early. Just when the press and other communications services were beginning to spell and pronounce his name correctly, and to realize that he wasn't Russian, Vukovich retreated and hid.

He ignored the entreaties of American race promoters who wanted him to help build their gates. He wasn't interested. He could, if he wanted to, merely show up and discover early in the race that something was wrong with his car and bring it in, which another "500" winner or two had agreed to do. Bill wasn't interested in displaying himself that way, nor was he interested in the money.

For this attitude many a promoter, and an occasional race driver, called him ungrateful and complained, "Vukovich isn't doing anything for racing." The philosophy of championship racing in the United States is that the Indianapolis champion should spend the year after his triumph gracing every course, lending his prestige, accepting bids to speak at luncheon clubs, and accept endorsement opportunities. Bill, oblivious, considered his time his to do with as he wished. Nor was he interested in enjoying the spoils of celebrity as some other "500" winners had done, such as running out on hotel bills and poaching socially into other men's territories, including their wives or girlfriends.

→-←

Only one automobile contest intrigued him — the Pan-American Road Race. It was a tortuous, four-day stock car competition the length of Mexico that held danger and tragedy both for participants and spectators. He joined Bill Stroppe's Lincoln team and the Mexicans, like their neighbors across the Rio Grande also slow to understand him, referred to him as "The Crazy Russian." But the adventure was short-lived. Bill dropped out of the race the first day because of transmission trouble.

Once more he turned to Fred Gerhardt for business advice. Fred smiled and said first Bill needed to return his silver dollar. "Nothing doing," Bill said, "I gave that thing a 500-mile ride and I'm keeping it." Gerhardt helped him set up a trust fund program. Bill took his 40 percent share of the $89,496 out of the Indianapolis victory — approximately $35,800 — and invested a large chunk of it, allowing for Uncle Sam's slice of $12,000.

He frequently appeared at Gerhardt's extensive body shop in Fresno to borrow a steel stand so he could face valves. Fred kidded him, "Why don't you buy your own?" And Bill would reply, "Oh no; things are pretty rough." Gerhardt and his employee force couldn't suppress a smile each time. Bill always approached and departed without a "hello" or "goodbye." A very efficient man.

Keck took him aside after the excitement of the triumph had ebbed and, paternally, advised him to remain humble. Bill was incredulous. "Why would I have to change?" he said. "A man would have to start leading another life if he's going to try to be somebody he isn't."

He didn't even bother to formally assemble the mementoes of his victory; he merely piled them into a corner or into a drawer out of the way. He gave the handsome wristwatch he had won for earning the pole position to Keck.

Keck, tuned to big business and written agreements, asked Travers if he should offer Vukovich a contract for the next race. Jim was firm: "Don't offer him one; he'll just laugh at us and tear it up. I asked him during the New York trip if he would drive for us again in 1954 and Bill had said 'OK.'" Travers knew that was good enough.

One day Bill's reticent and independent nature got the best of him. The *Los Angeles Times* wanted him to represent auto racing at its annual banquet of champions, an impressive, well-attended, well-publicized affair assembling titular heads of numerous sports. The sponsors asked Agajanian to approach Bill. Reluctantly, Bill agreed. He even bought a smart new gray flannel suit to wear.

The day of the banquet he and Esther drove down to Los Angeles from Fresno. They arrived in the afternoon with time on their hands. He suggested to Esther they go visit Travers in Beverly Hills first. The three talked on and on. Bill was aware the time was slipping away, but he was enjoying being with his buddy and was nervous about the evening's engagement. So, he didn't go, and wasn't honored, and the racing brass felt he had let them down again and the press continued to call him difficult to understand, and the *Times* people were angry.

While he continued biding his time, Hollywood called. The producers of a race picture — "Roar of the Crowd" — wanted real drivers as extras, at $250 a week. Bill went for three days but the glamour didn't impress him and the economics didn't figure. "Hell," he said, "with all your living expenses up there, it wasn't worth it, just to be able to say you were in the damn movies."

Almost daily he sought the company of his Fresno coffee companions, usually walking the mile — bright and early — to their favorite diner hangout, Carol's. Some days he would stop at brother Mike's automotive service shop to help Mike on jobs. "You change spark plugs," he said. "I'll do the heavy stuff."

The next 500-Mile Race was never far from his thoughts, and he continued to feel that time was terribly short. He kept bicycling and doing pushups. And walking, always walking.

As spring bloomed, he found succor for his restlessness in young Billy's entry into Little League baseball. The boy was playing with a battle-worn glove, and he ventured to ask his dad if he could have a new one. Bill bargained with him. If he could make the first team, he would get his new glove. Young Billy accepted the terms without comment and walked away. When the team was picked, he approached his father. "Well, you better take me downtown," he said.

Proud Dad bought not only the new $11 mitt but added a pair of spiked shoes.

And then, just before the exodus to Indianapolis, he decided he'd better sharpen his reflexes. He entered a midget race at Gardena and won the pole. In the trophy dash Parsons flipped and scraped along on the track upside down. He needed forty stitches to sew up his left shoulder. It was questionable now whether Parsons could mend in time to participate in the 1954 "500." In the minutes before the main event, Bill sat deep in thought. Travers, a spectator, told him it wasn't worth the ride with so little at stake. Johnnie, too, was a "500" winner, but mostly bad luck dogged his trail after his victory. Vukovich had his triumph, the biggest payday Indianapolis ever saw, his health, a loving family, a rosy future. And with each race the law of averages draws closer to each driver.

The $500 appearance money was good, but … he pulled out of the feature event.

He rendezvoused with Bob Veith and they set sail on the 2,500 mile trip to Indianapolis — first stopping at Oklahoma City for a 100-lap midget race both had entered. The event was rained out, postponed to the next day. Bill fretted. Rain brought another postponement. Bill could stand it no longer. Appearance money or not, he left Veith and Oklahoma City. He had to get to Indianapolis, even though it was only the first of May.

He had something to prove again, and he couldn't wait.

8

"A man can win this race from any position."

Middle of the Pack

Vukovich was not so frustrated as the month began at the Speedway. The routine was the same, leaving the Thompson home early and spending the day at the track. But he talked to more people, sat still more often, smiled more often and appeared more relaxed. He even played gin rummy — the favorite driver rainy-day diversion — in the garage area cafeteria, holding his cards in those knotty-muscled hands, obviously inexperienced — like a boy handling his first cigarette. But he played with typical concentration, setting his own pace despite heckling, and he gave back as much as he got. And he won, too.

He still looked hungry in a race car, and he still tormented Travers and Coon. "Butchers," he called them whenever the machine wasn't functioning as it should, and for a final jab he would point to a picture of his own wonderful midget, "Old Ironsides," and allow as how he had kept *it* running perfectly.

He would steal away to the southwest corner of the grounds, near the first turn, to scout other drivers' techniques coming out of the main straight. "You gotta see how the other guys are going through," he said. Asked why he bothered, he said, "You're never too old to learn." He regarded straightaway speed, even at 170 mph, as relatively unimportant. "My grandmother can come down these chutes," he said. "You gotta crank the damn thing around the turns to get around here fast."

He and his crew had the car, now three years old, ready early and spectators and rivals stopped conversations and turned to watch him when he climbed in for practice runs. He was the man to beat, all figured, and he instilled a mixture of respect and fear, evidenced by the unusually muted tones of crews operating in the pit area near him and by the rush to the pit wall of fans who thrilled at watching him take a car around the track.

Others showed faster early speed through practice days plagued by cold and rain, but on May 8th he climbed to top rehearsal honors with a 134.7 clocking. He told Travers and Coon, "It feels lovely. Don't change anything."

He gruffly turned down public appearance requests unless he would be paid, and the drivers who knew of his secret generosity chuckled at this hard pose. Aware of the picture he painted of himself, he used Mauri Rose as an illustration of the man who was a right guy but who was generally criticized for aloofness. He liked to tell the story of the time someone yelled to Rose to come meet a friend and Mauri had yelled in return: "Hell, no! I know too many people now!"

But Bill never passed anyone — especially youngsters — waiting at a fence with a scrap of paper in his hand for an autograph, although many other drivers walked on.

In the privacy of the garage, he received no more reverence from the crew than he gave the crew, which now had something of a corner on the brains market, having added Jack Beckley, who had been McGrath's mechanic. They wanted to know what Bill had done with his money. Had he buried it in cans in his backyard? Bill said he had invested it in something with 7 percent interest. "You can't beat that, can you? You can always spend the damned stuff. So, I'm holding on to it."

He expressed regret at standing up the *Los Angeles Times* party. "I was wrong. A guy shouldn't do that. I told the guy I was going to be there. But I got talking to Smoky (Travers) and I just let it go. A guy shouldn't do that after he's promised. Boy, I was wrong there … especially if I'd a called they coulda got someone else."

And he exercised, as before. It wasn't unusual to see him walking briskly in the garage area and then suddenly stop, feet apart, hands behind back, and stare straight ahead, absorbed in thought.

One day the pit wall repartee was especially sharp as drivers waited for mechanics to finish chores. Tony Bettenhausen held out a pair of goggles toward Bill, saying, "Here's the best damned goggle ever made, Vuk."

Bill replied: "Hell, I don't need 'em. I hit the wall in a two-bit pair of goggles. What you need is a pair that makes those turns look bigger."

Cal Niday improved on it. "What you need is a pair that straightens those curves out."

The Keck Kids progress was smooth and two days before the beginning of qualifications Bill turned an easy 137.1 for the fourth fastest practice lap. That night with Esther he made an uncomfortable appearance at an informal press dinner to receive the L. Strauss & Co. award — an oil painting of himself — for winning the '53 race. Throughout the meal, ill at ease, he had little to say, and just before the presentation was to be made, he excused himself and asked me to accompany him.

Bill wanted me to check his acceptance speech. "I don't like these affairs," he said. "If I could talk, I wouldn't mind." I assured him the response he planned was fine, and by way of putting him at ease, complimented him on the handsome gray flannel suit. Bill was not too nervous to reply, dryly. "I bought this for another banquet," he said, referring to the one he skipped in Los Angeles. "Boy, were they happy!"

A few moments later he did so well with his acceptance as to prompt *The Indianapolis News* sports editor Bill Fox to write the next day that Bill had accepted the award "... in gracious manner and typical of his boyish simplicity expressed his appreciation to the donors of the trophy ... and with a twinkle in his eye told (the artist) he did a 'pretty good paint job.'"

＊-＊

And then suddenly, the day before the trials, a maelstrom of activity for everyone, the Kecks found trouble. Somehow, they had lost horsepower. From an easy 137 mph Vukovich was now straining all out to reach 133. Ruttman, on one occasion, went sailing by him.

The pit area was a madhouse of engines, whistling guards and scurrying crew members. The Kecks, no longer dominating, hurried away with their car, pushed it into the garage and locked the doors. The crew tore it down excitedly. Bill paced in anguish.

Seldom at the Speedway does a minute go by that a camera doesn't click. Now someone was inspired to assemble an unusually large number of former winners entered in the race for a group picture. The other four — Parsons (his lame shoulder improving), Holland, Ruttman and Wallard — were rounded up quickly and a battery of photographers formed just as fast, for no cameraman's idea remains exclusive for long at the Speedway. Then a brave emissary was sent to talk Vukovich into the plan. Surprisingly, he agreed — on the promise that the foolishness would be brief. The promise was made. Bill tried in the first few shots to keep up a smile, but it rapidly faded, though the others grinned broadly. Bill snapped, "C'mon, take the damned picture; I've got work to do!" An impromptu bull session developed between the crowd of onlookers and the other champs when the photographers were done, but Bill wordlessly battled his way through and returned to the garage.

Now he looked even more worried than Travers. "Maybe you've got cockpit trouble," he offered, blaming himself for the slowing speeds. But the crew thought the pistons were at fault; they were throwing oil through the breathers, as was happening with some other cars. Where the engine used to power 5,200 rpm, now it could get only 4,500.

Travers was defiant. "We'll get it licked, by God." He turned to Bill: "When Ruttman doubled you up, I was so embarrassed I wanted to hide."

Bill felt the same: "When he went by me so fast, I waved and shut off as if I was coming in.

"Smoky, I was going flat out and turning just 4,500. That's an awful feeling." He said it almost sadly and Travers answered, sympathetically.

"Yeh, I know."

Keck was on the phone from California. Travers told him their troubles and promised: "We're going to do our damndest to qualify tomorrow."

They worked all evening and all night, until 5 in the morning, and they still didn't know. A warm, sunny day dawned. Bill sneaked in a practice turn ten minutes before the official track open and the car still was not quite right. A line of cars formed to await qualifying. A steady stream of attempts began. Three broke Chet Miller's track record and the redoubtable McGrath — his own mechanic now — cut the fastest ones of all, a 141.287 single lap with a 141.033 four-lap average speed. The Kecks, fighting drowsiness, debated what to do as qualified cars mounted up.

They had a dilemma. Should they go ahead and attempt qualification this first day and get whatever speed they could, then have the remainder of the month to prepare the car? Or, tear it down now and find the trouble and not let Bill try to make up what the car lacked and risk injury? Their pride wouldn't let them make any bid but their best and they valued Bill's safety. So, forsaking the advantages of first-day qualifying — while their rivals and the 120,000 customers, the largest time trial throng in history, wondered where they were — they decided to dismantle it completely. Every nut and bolt.

They had begun the day angry and anxious, but they gradually grew subdued. At 7:00 that evening they began to smile and joke. "After a while," Beckley said, "you get silly."

Even Smoky had an occasional gag, but he continued working. "I never saw a more beautiful day in Indiana," Beckley observed once, and Travers added, "Yeh, but a tragic day."

Even Bill eventually simmered down and began to talk of taking Esther out to dinner. "The hell with qualifying today," he said, "the thing to do is get in the race and run hell out of them in the race."

Thirteen drivers qualified that day. That was at least thirteen that Vukovich would have to overcome in the race. Nine had averaged more than 138 mph. *The Indianapolis Star* next morning asked: "Which way did Bill Vukovich go?"

At 4 p.m. the next day, after three more had qualified before rain stopped the trials, the Keck Kids were back in business. The car was in one piece again, after sixty consecutive hours of work, with new engine block, pistons, and rods. During the night part of the crew had driven to Lowell, Ind., 140 miles north, for the pistons and had returned at 3 in the morning. The engine now had been torn down and reassembled twice in two days.

Immediate problems solved, thoughts turned elsewhere. "Well, if we get some good weather now, we may see a miracle," Travers said. Hilborn sat down to copy the competition's chute speeds. Driving philosophy had changed at Indianapolis. Now it was not so much driving deep down the chutes — "to the gate" — it was taking the curves faster.

By now it was becoming obvious some of Vukovich's racing foes had become jealous of his success. He couldn't understand why, having never experienced envy.

"A lot of guys are bitter," he said, "I don't begrudge 'em anything. If a guy can do something, more power to him. Everybody's got the same chance."

He quickly changed the subject to Billy and his Little League baseball career, his success in school, and his lack of interest in becoming a race driver. A favorite story concerned the boy's craftiness in tricking the teacher into calling on him after she had begun to ignore his constantly raised hand. Young Bill would feign inattentiveness — and then get called on. Dad smiled warmly telling it.

Despite their heroic efforts the rain washed away hopes for qualifying on Sunday. Now they must wait and wonder. The very next day was perfect for practice, but they received another jolt. In one last look at the engine, they discovered that the new block they had installed had a sand hole in a cylinder. The cylinder was full of water. There was the thinnest of silver linings to their plight; had Bill taken out the car the engine could have been ruined. Nothing to be done now except to make a hurry-up call to California for a new block and rebuild once more. Dame Fortune never stays permanently in the same garage, and she snubs rich as well as poor.

Much of the talk around the Speedway the ensuing week was about McGrath's practice times. On one fuel test he averaged 137.8 for forty miles. When a radio man asked if that was the pace he intended for the race, Jack answered innocently, "Well, I was running pretty easy."

In a later interview McGrath gave no mileage details but did say: "I hope to go into that first turn first and if I do the rest of the fellows are going to have a chase on their hands."

Not until Friday, the day before the last weekend of qualifying, was Bill able to step into the car. He stood on the throttle and, amazingly, reached 140 mph. The Kecks seemed, not an hour too soon, ready to defend their laurels. But Travers, chastened by all the mechanical misfortune they had endured, did not exult: "We'd just like to get in the race, but you know him. He wants to set a record." Then as an afterthought, Travers added: "I'd like to have the record, too."

Ideal weather the next day did not ease the tension at the track, for there were seventeen places left to fill and time was short. For the unqualified drivers and many of the fans, it felt like race day itself.

Bill greeted the day with a smile and claimed to feel OK, but Beckley reported he had just seen him carrying a cup of coffee and was "shaking so bad he spilled it all over his hand."

But later in some pit-wall byplay, as qualifying approached, Bill thrust out his hands with other drivers to determine whose nerves were the most controlled. His were completely steady.

He lined up third to qualify, but the man before him spun emerging from the first turn an incredible seven times without hitting anything. The last two loops were below the track and spewed dirt onto the course. Vukovich had to wait, strapped in the car, while a cleanup crew made the track safe again.

He sat completely relaxed with a faint smile that at times shaded nearly to a smirk, as if he were ridiculing the unwanted solicitude around him. A swarm of track officials and many with no business there at all clucked around him, less in pursuit of duties than to crowd into the spotlight surrounding him. He talked easily with the flag-waver, Seth Klein, through the twenty-minute delay.

He was pushed onto the track to applause — there were 50,000 in the stands and along the fences — and his first lap around was only a slow warm-up. But as he appeared the second time, he held his hand high in the air; he wanted the green flag. The first lap was 139.578. The second dropped to 138.249. The third leveled off at 138.355. The fourth dropped again, to 137.74. The average four lap speed was 138.478, almost three mph slower than McGrath.

He wore a dejected expression when he drove to a halt in front of his crew. "Did we do 138?" he asked. The crew members were cloaked in disappointment but also showed a measure of relief. They had been bucking bad luck for a long time, but at least they were in the race. "It's been a long worry," Travers murmured.

There was no jostling scramble by outsiders toward their garage this time. The fickle crowd leaves if you are not running in front. Bill managed a grin that had an apology written in it. His crew hastened to comfort him.

"That's a load off our mind," Coon offered. "We're in the race."

"Hell, there were times I thought we'd never get this far," Travers said.

"Was that sand and stuff bothering you?" Beckley asked.

"Hell no," Bill answered. "I was all over the track. I made two good turns. Hell, in that southwest turn four guys could have gone underneath me. I almost lost it once down there."

When the day had quieted and afternoon gave way to evening, he confessed he had started to spin in the third turn on one lap.

"Boy, I gave those Triple-A guys a thrill," he said, referring to the officials from the race's governing body, the American Automobile Association, who were stationed around the track at various posts. "I had 'em phoning all over the place. I sent a couple of guys heading for the pea patches. When you're going so sloppy, you're riding in your own dust, you're terrible … I couldn't have broken that record today. I wasn't kidding myself … But I'll clue you; this baby (the car) can do it."

And then, talking more to himself than to his audience, he added, more quietly: "I just never convinced myself."

Travers refused to be downhearted, though it was obvious the machine wasn't right and they were going to be buried deep in the field; six other drivers that day were faster than Bill.

"I said this morning I'd be glad when this day is over and I am," Travers said.

Wallard entered, his eyes glistening, and walked close to Bill. His tone was full of sympathy and affection. "Vuky, if you don't do any good in this race, don't feel bad, 'cause you won her once."

He turned and started away. Bill let him get to the door, then called after him dryly: "Where'd you get the beer?"

That evening Bill stretched out on a couch at the Thompsons, breathed a huge sigh of relief, and said, "I'm glad the pressure is off." Even Esther was surprised by his reaction.

✦✦

Qualifications ended the following day in a wild, improbable, nerve-wracking, pressure-packed session. During its warm, sunlit hours many a man sees his toil and sweat go for naught and his high-risk gamble of money and effort fail in the face of competition, time, and an unwilling machine.

Indianapolis continually provides a new form of heartbreak, and this time young, likeable Bob Scott was picked for an unusual twist of fate.

Scott had appeared at the Speedway two years earlier with $25 to his name and he lived on it through the month of May. It was still a struggle to maintain his family on his race earnings. This last day, after being bumped from the field, he seemed about to get back into it in another car, just minutes before qualification deadline — 6 p.m. His first three laps were sufficiently fast, but then, inexplicably, he shut off the engine.

To his horror he realized too late that he had, in his excitement, mistaken the white last-lap flag for the checkered and had misinterpreted a friend's exuberant shaking fist. Bob Sweikert had meant, *You're doing fine.* Scott interpreted the salute as, *You're finished.* He had stopped too soon.

And so Scott, a poor man in a dangerous profession, cried a long time and apologized to many he thought he had let down. He wanted no one to blame Sweikert, only himself.

Elisian made a successful rookie debut, surviving a historic bumping session that even knocked out Nalon and a Novi by qualifying another car into the last row. The finest equipment in history combined to produce a record average of 138.632 mph.

Vukovich's speed was below the average, and he was buried in the nineteenth spot, in the seventh row. It had been eighteen years since anyone had won the race from that deep in the field. For the past seven years no winner had begun farther back than seventh, in the third row. It would take a miracle to overcome the crowd of drivers ahead of him.

❧·❦

By happenstance of the calendar, eight days remained before the running of the race, providing endless time for opportunities. Especially in the press. The majority of the writers covering the Speedway were impressed with McGrath's superlative speed — 1.2 mph faster than anyone else — and easy operation which, they reasoned, foretold a smooth race effort. His cooperative, personable manner also contributed to their designation of him as the favorite. Vukovich, they believed, not only was too far back in the pack but the odds against consecutive victories were too great. Only two men had ever accomplished that feat — Wilbur Shaw and Mauri Rose. Besides, his crew was struggling with his car, a harbinger of failure for the demanding journey of 500 miles. In fact, by race day the Keck Kids had stripped and refitted their ailing automobile seven times, a remarkable display of tenacity by them — and stubbornness on the part of the machine.

But Bill's message was beginning to reach the newsmen. They, in turn, had begun to understand him, resenting less his independence and, in fact, grinning about it. Even envying him for it. They couldn't quite imagine him fighting all the way up to the front against such odds, but they also didn't believe they could afford to ignore him entirely.

One Indianapolis race writer picked a top three finish of McGrath, Vukovich and Rodger Ward, in that order. Another predicted McGrath, to be followed by Chuck Stevenson and Duane Carter. One bold headline read: "McGrath Is Man to Beat In '500.'" The form chart of the *News* favored the three Bardahl cars, driven by Sam Hanks, the current AAA driving champion; Jim Rathmann; and Art Cross, who had been second in '53 at 6-1 odds. It further prophesied that any one of the three was capable of winning, calling Hanks and his "wonderful car" the "smoothest combination imaginable."

Vukovich was picked at 7-1, McGrath at 8-1. The chart read: "Hanks starts in a cozy position, inside on the fourth row, and can maneuver to his liking … Bill Vukovich? The Terrible Slovenian will be much irked at starting so far back from those succulent lap prizes, but he can be counted on to move up through sheer determination … The reason he isn't the favorite is that his car has had spells of sickness, and that whoever turns the wheels of destiny has a way of taking care of boys who get more than their share of money at the Speedway. The sleeping law of averages awakens and asserts itself."

One of the newsmen asked Ruttman, "Do you think anyone will catch McGrath?"

"Yes. Billy Vukovich. You mark my words, when fifteen laps are run Vukovich is going to be knocking on any man's door who is up there in front."

"What does Vuky have, Troy?"

"Determination, hustle, brains. Fight! He'll never give up and he's in condition. I know. I've known the man for a long time."

Precedent, percentages and the law of averages got no concession from Vukovich. When asked, "What are your chances?" he answered with a slight sneer: "A man can win this race from any position."

⋙⋘

At dinner at Hollyhock Hill two nights before the race with my wife and me, Esther asked if I had seen the morning *Star's* selection of McGrath to win, with Vukovich second.

Bill cut in, harshly: "If they'd pay me off second-place money right now I wouldn't take it!"

Bill's eyes were flashing, his chin raised, and he brandished a fork for emphasis. The conversation paused. Second place would be worth at least $30,000. His meaning was clear. He wanted to race for all of it.

I told him Ruttman had predicted he would be fighting for the lead inside fifteen laps. Bill opened his mouth, ready to talk of his plans, but immediately snapped it shut. "I don't want to crow before the race. The time to crow is afterwards — and then you shouldn't."

That finished all conversation about the race among the four of us as Bill lapsed into a carefree recitation of the latest news he and Esther had heard from the children. Marlene had recently written, "Dear Daddy, blow those hot-dogs off the track." Bill chuckled happily, repeating it.

He was comfortable in the restaurant's homey, uncrowded dining room, a converted homestead on the north outskirts of Indianapolis. The waitresses, courteous, attractive young women dressed in Colonial period dresses, eventually recognized him, and shyly approached him for autographs as we made ready to leave. He was pleased, but even more timid than they as he signed his name.

"I've got a bull of a man, haven't I."

Hard Earned Victory

At the drivers' meeting the day before the race Bill was the last to appear. The day was muggy with a brilliant, thirsty sun. The Pagoda lawn, scene of the meeting, was stampeded by a half-hundred fans toting cameras, trained first on the drivers then on the lead visiting celebrity — actress Marie Wilson, selected the Bullpen hostess this year.

Addressing the drivers, Wilson began with a rehearsed joke but, touched by the tension the approach of race day brings, she ended with a plea: "I've been a clown all my life, so it's kind of hard to be serious. But God loves us all equally. Don't try to kill each other trying to be first tomorrow. God bless you all and good luck."

Later that evening the Keck Kids practiced pit changes. They completed one in just thirty-two seconds, refueling in only sixteen.

One hour and 15 minutes before the race was to roll into its flying start — with, naturally, a warm, sunny day on hand — Vukovich was at peace. It was in sharp contrast to the previous year. He paced up and down the pit area, out of habit, but there was no impatience in his stride, and he even snapped his fingers lightheartedly as he walked. But as the minutes swept by the new smile began to recede into the old set face. When the first bomb went off and the sound of "Taps" was heard, fifteen minutes before the start, it was the old Vukovich.

Jim Nairn, who was still in engineering school, attempted a light sendoff: "Hey Smoky, earn us a scholarship."

It was just the right touch for the crew. Everyone grinned. Bill replied wryly: "I'll be thinking of that while we're running. Something to keep me happy." Then, keeping with the spirit of the moment, he asked Nairn: "Want to ride with me, Jim?"

The ten-minute bomb startled them and prompted Coon to remark, in the tension: "That's good for the nerves."

With just minutes remaining, Bill, in the reflex that often occurs to the man trying hard to get his breath just before the battle, yawned. A minute remaining, he lifted his leg over the side of the cockpit.

Travers, crabby Travers, was moved to sentiment. He leaned over in the cockpit:

"Well, Bill, we've had some disagreements, but it's all forgotten."

"You butchers haven't done a damned thing!" Bill shot back. He couldn't be sentimental at so grim a moment, lest softness undo him.

→←

It was McGrath, of course, leading the first lap. Also, the second and the third. But by the fifth lap Vukovich, who had started nineteenth, was eleventh. He gained four more spots on the following lap. But by now he had caught the fastest cars and the toughest competitors. At the eleventh lap he was eighth and closing in on Hanks. Up front, Bryan was challenging McGrath and third came Ruttman in a mad charge. Troy had been promised $1,000 by his car owner for every lap he could lead before the twentieth, and he was driving as if in a wild trance.

Fourth was Johnny Thomson, fifth Jimmy Daywalt, sixth Cross and then Hanks. A lunging surge and Bill went by Hanks. But it wasn't going to be that easy. Hanks, his car superior in the turns and off corners because of its lower gear, got back around. Then began a fierce battle for that patch of track both wanted, a duel so tense the 175,000 spellbound viewers turned their eyes from the front runners to watch the gray No. 14 dog the black No. 1.

At hell-bent speed, Vukovich probed here, probed there. Hanks, wary and experienced, cut him off and slid in front of him, blocking him in every attempt to pass. Bill increased the pressure. He moved his car closer and closer to Hanks. In the stands Esther, though fearful, managed a smile to herself. She knew this was when Bill loved it the most, relentlessly applying his nerve against the man in front of him, challenging him to show a later breaking point.

Once, Vukovich edged his car's nose underneath Hanks. But there was so little room that Bill's right front tire touched Sam's left rear and a tiny, black puff of smoke popped into the air at the contact of two churning tires, a split second from calamity.

Up in the press box atop a grandstand a veteran race historian typed: "… a brutal thing was taking place. Vukovich was charging Hanks. That Vukovich is a master race driver no one can deny. He tailed Hanks, the national champion. On one turn he would ride high and almost pass. On the next he would go inside. Then, for a full lap not six inches separated tail and radiator. Hanks' head swiveled from side to side. Vukovich was determined to put this driver out of the race. There is no mental or physical torture any worse than bulldogging. The trick originated during the board-track days. Vukovich was playing the modern version and no man alive could stand up to it for long."

Vukovich broke through Hanks on Lap 37 and found himself fourth in the race, behind McGrath, Baywalt, and Cross. The blistering pace — an incredible 139.860 mph at twenty laps — had dropped Thomson behind; scorched tires sent Ruttman and Bryan to the pits early. Then McGrath himself had to come in on Lap 44, moving Daywalt, Cross and Vukovich up. Daywalt and Cross alternated leads, with Vukovich gaining on them.

Pit stops now became rampant, including Daywalt and Cross, and Vukovich found himself leading the race on Lap 60. The miracle was an illusion, however. He had only that brief circuit, for he also had to come in for four new tires and refueling. He yelled for a second cup of water and poured it down his back. Travers had trouble locking the gas cap, but the crew was able to send him on his way in forty-two seconds.

The wholesale stops, of varying duration, now had the scorers confused and positions were nearly guesswork until the electric scoring tape could be deciphered and standings posted. By Lap 72 all cars were back on the track again and the race once more presented true positions:

Bryan first, then McGrath, Vukovich, Daywalt, all in the same lap, with Ruttman pushing hard a lap behind.

On Lap 88, however, Bryan had to pull his valiant little dirt track car back into the pits. Now Vukovich had only one man left in front of him, McGrath, riding in the record-breaker. Bill seemed to be imposing his will on his automobile and now was challenging for the lead.

Lap by lap he closed the gap steadily. They came down the main straightaway to finish the ninety-first. Exhilarated, thousands strained to watch as Vukovich darted past. He was in the clear. Not yet half the race was run, and he had pulled himself up from what history for eighteen years had decreed was an impossible position. He hadn't won yet but had accomplished one miracle. He was in front. The burden was now on his chasers.

The gas cap that Travers had found balky now became unbuttoned and it bobbed up and down just behind Bill's head. He ignored it and continued his even driving. He no longer bullied the car but took it as uniformly through the turns as did any of the artists.

Now pit stops came rapidly, not for the sake of the automobiles but for relief of drivers in the humid, 89-degree temperature. An inordinate amount of substituting was taking place, more, even, than in the year before. With fresh pilots being thrust into cars, up and down the pits it looked like a battle between Vukovich and all the manpower the other crews could muster. But Bill continued to mount seconds to his lead each time around, though part of his margin was wiped out when Daywalt and Pat Flaherty tangled and forced thirteen minutes under the yellow light. Then, as McGrath attempted to leave his pit, his engine stalled and Bryan assumed second place.

A refueling and tire-changing pause was coming soon for Vukovich and what the Keck Kids did with it could determine whether he would maintain command the remainder of the way. Bill, an eye on the left rear tread, chose the 128th lap. But the Agajanian crew, in the pit immediately in front of him, had its car in, too. It was lined up badly, its tail protruding excessively. A shallow entry for Bill was impossible. He would have to make two sharp turns, left and right, to align squarely in his allotted area. Barreling in and faced with the necessity of readjusting his speed instantly, he yanked left, then quickly right, but he had gone in too deep, and the left front wheel banged into and nestled against the wall.

The Keck crew had split-second decisions to make. Push him back and try to line him up nearly parallel with the wall? Or just back far enough to slide the manual roll jack under both front tires? Jim Nairn, the front wheel man, made up his mind instantly. He remembered how well the left front tire had held up last year. He reasoned it would survive. He slipped the jack to the left and hoisted only the right front for the change. Hilborn swiftly calculated fuel consumption and shouted to Travers to fill the tank completely, that Bill could go the remaining seventy-two laps with it. Tires generally were expended at a three-stop rate, so crews had been filling tanks only partially, to spare the driver from handling extra weight. But the Kecks calculated they could make it to the finish in two stops.

During the sixty-one seconds the crew scrambled, the spontaneous sportsmanship that often flashes through the Speedway emerged. Travers, because the car was slightly out of position, couldn't reach the fuel tank mouth with the hose, but Johnnie Parsons, out of the race, and one of his crew members standing behind the pit hurled themselves at the ponderous, pressurized fuel storage cylinder and nudged it forward. From the pit on the other side of Vukovich, driver Ray Crawford reached over the wall to hand Bill a second cup of water. When Bill was gone again, Agajanian apologized for his obstructive auto.

Straw asked Nairn: "Did you get a good look at the tire? Can it last?"

He replied: 'Yes I did, but he hit the wall so hard I don't know what he did to the tire."

The long stop had sent Bryan ahead and now Vukovich had to prove himself again. Bryan was going to have to pit again but Bill was impatient to catch up. He gained time steadily. Bryan, though, was driving a car with a broken rear spring and a broken front shock absorber. He came in on the 148th lap and it was Vukovich's race again.

Second by second Bill padded his margin on Bryan, with Ruttman now third and McGrath fourth. Only the gamble on the tires threatened him and with thirty-five laps remaining his crew warned him on the signal board: "EZ" "TYRS."

A huge, black cloud had formed in the southwest and dust-filled gusts were beginning to blow across the southern fringe of the track.

Bill kept widening the distance, leading on the 180th lap by fifty-nine seconds. Now he had Bryan in sight up ahead. Coon signaled him, palms undulating toward the ground, to slow down. Meanwhile, a crew member flashed him the board, begging: "EZ." Still he came on, going for Bryan. The crew tried a calculating approach: "Hold 9," they signaled, meaning keep Bryan in sight and finish it that way.

Suddenly, on Lap 184, the black cloud burst in the southeast turn and the rain and wind caused Pat O'Connor to spin. He was unhurt and the Kecks breathed a sigh of relief as the cars slowed under the yellow light. Their chauffeur began riding with his left arm resting on the side of the cockpit like a Sunday driver out in his convertible. If any of the other crews had remaining doubts that Vukovich could go all the way with just that second pit stop, they vanished with that picture of him at his ease. Aggie stepped over to shake Travers' hand, but Jim refused.

"Not yet, Ag." Then he smiled. "We'll know for sure later."

The race resumed on Lap 188. The Keck crew still had to convince Vukovich to remain cautious. Once more, the "Hold 9" sign. But even as they gave it, Vukovich, still competing, went belligerently by Bryan.

He had been calculating his own strategy.

First, he knew scoring a four-hour race for 200 laps for so many cars could produce (and had in the past) miscounts. Maybe just one lap, but if the mistake was to include him, he wanted that extra lap on the second-place man in his favor. He could still win by a car length.

Second, if Bryan were to spin in front of him, he might become involved and be deprived of victory. He knew what last-minute tricks fate could play.

Third, there was a psychological advantage to a show of superiority. If once more he went by Bryan, he might finally convince Jimmy of the futility of the chase and thus make the last laps easier for himself.

"We can't slow him down," Hilborn muttered.

Now a chilling demonstration of the grueling demands of the race took place. The No. 1 Bardahl car came roaring down the main straightaway, its crankshaft broken, thus locking its rear wheels, and slid spectacularly for 300 yards. Who was to say that the tremendous pressure Vukovich had put on Bardahl and Hanks earlier hadn't contributed to that breakdown?

It took the checkered flag to slow down Vukovich. He finished with a little wave of his left arm to the fans as his concession to race winner convention. His speed average was 130.840 mph, the fastest the 500 miles had ever been run. There had been twenty-seven driver changes, with only McGrath and Vukovich going solo all the way. Now Vukovich had led 435 of the 600 laps over three years, the most concentrated superiority in the history of the race. Ralph DePalma with 613 total laps led and Shaw with 508 still ranked above him, but DePalma had participated in ten Indianapolis races, Shaw in thirteen. Vukovich had now been in but four.

Up in the press box and throughout the Speedway grounds, journalists and fans alike enthused over the tremendous combat. One thought intruded — that this had become primarily an event of and for men, now a shade more important than the cars, as it should be. And at the head of the pack was an awesomely determined human who seemed hell-bent on making the race his own.

Bill endured the Bullpen again, bracing himself against all the questions and commands from reporters and photographers. He enjoyed the traditional kiss from the Hollywood actress, grinning at his crew while their lips were pressed together. Marie Wilson, meanwhile, closed her eyes in the accepted Hollywood fashion. Then he kissed her again, for those inevitable cameramen who never have confidence in their first focus. He even smiled a couple of times.

The Indianapolis Star's account described the scene: "The frog that habitually lies in Vuky's throat was given water next. With the dust rinsed from vocal cords, Vuky became talkative to the extent of saying, 'I'm the luckiest guy in the world again.' Vuky's mechanic, Jim Travers, shook his head at that. 'That wasn't luck,' Travers said. 'There's the greatest race driver in the United States in that car.' Then a young reporter

Another victory, two more kisses. This time from Esther and Marie Wilson. (IMS Photos)

asked Vuky a superfluous question: 'Did you just press down hard and keep going?' Vuky snorted. 'What else?'"

Esther later confessed she had expected McGrath to win.

"He's so sweet and gentle," Marie Wilson said as Vukovich bolted the enclosure to hew a path back to the garage.

While this was going on, Bryan, a 6-foot 200-pounder whose great strength was all that kept him going on such a hot day in a misbehaving car, lay collapsed on his garage floor, skin peeled off his back and hands. He hovered on the borderline of consciousness for nearly five minutes. Then his lips moved: "Well, he beat me."

Escorted by Speedway guards, Bill made his way to the garage. A rapidly growing crowd fell in behind him until it was held back by the

The newspaper headline tells the story while Speedway president Wilbur Shaw specifies the victory total. (IMS Photos)

rope and the doors. He continued into a corner and the crew left him alone. Laboriously, he pulled off shoes, then stockings. The left heel was blistered again this year. He sat back and placed a wet washcloth on his head.

"Feel OK, Smoky?" Travers called over.

He had to repeat it. Bill had been deafened. But this time he looked up.

"Yeah."

Esther, only just now having caught up again, entered. "I've got a bull of a man, haven't I," she said on her way to Bill.

The car? The left front tire, despite having gone 140 laps, looked better than the right front. Bill paid tribute to the pistons, which had been much of their worriment throughout May, and Travers agreed, saying, "I'm going to frame those pistons in gold." The crew quickly pulled a canvas over the machine, blocking the prying, knowledgeable eyes that might spot some of their ideas.

There was more interviewing to be done for the public address system and radio stations. Bill enjoyed a little joke as he answered the inevitable question about comparing the two victories: "Last year was harder. It was so hot. This year was nice and cool."

Between interviews he made an extravagant routine out of smoking a huge cigar someone had given him, to the amusement of the insiders now gathered in the garage. Several of his rivals' wives accompanied their congratulations with a kiss.

Bryan's mechanic, Clint Brawner, approached, hand out and smiling. "Glad you got second. Maybe you should have won," Bill said. Brawner replied: "No. You earned it." Ruttman came, shouting, "I'm happy for you!" and then added quietly, "Who did I tell you would win? He's the greatest."

To one radio broadcaster, who asked if he was worried during the race, Bill said laconically, "I just kept running to see what would happen." And to another, "I plan to drive a couple more years here anyway."

In another part of the garage, mechanic Harry Stephens, whose three favored Bardahl cars had used seven different drivers, said, "You have to hand it to that Vukovich. He's a he-man."

Esther takes a seat in the winning car with another instant newspaper headline celebrating her "bull of a man." (IMS Photos)

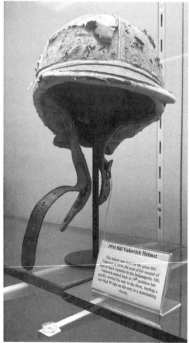

Above: Finally free of the masses, Vukovich recovers from another hard-won race. (IMS Photos)

Left: The helmet Vukovich wore on his way to his 1954 victory, as displayed in the Indianapolis Motor Speedway Museum. (Photo by Mark Montieth)

The next day in Nashville, the *Tennessean* newspaper reported: "Bill Vukovich won ... because he was the most stubborn and best-conditioned driver in Indianapolis." In Boston, the *Globe* account read: "Bill earned his victory the hard way." The *Detroit News* correspondent sent: "He won the fiercest and the fastest 500-Mile Race of all time ... the 35-year-old Californian, feared by every one of his thirty-two rivals ... proved he could fight his way from behind." *The Courier-Journal* in Louisville reported: "The swarthy Slovenian ... drove ... to absolute supremacy over thirty-two other hard-charging drivers." And, *The Commercial-Appeal* from Memphis had it: "'Wait for me, Wild Bill,' was a futile plea this sun-spangled and rain-haunted Monday as Mr. William Vukovich, an impatient Slav, won his second 500-Mile joust."

The galloping journalism even produced — surprisingly — a Vukovich byline story in *The Indianapolis Times*. The assignment began with little hope by the city desk and not much eagerness from the reporter, who had been warned about Bill's dislike for his kind. But Bill accepted him with a shrug and while slouched in a chair spiced the conversation with powerful profanity. After a bit the reporter said he wanted to print some of Bill's choicest words. Bill hesitated a second or two, then said, "Go ahead, say anything you want." Bystanders had gathered around and began pumping Bill, and the reporter grew fearful the whole thing would blow up. Bill, chatting easily before the crowd had formed, now grew restless.

He stayed, however, and the reporter warmed to him, even getting the feeling they were becoming friends. When he suggested using Bill's name in an as-told-to byline there was another pause. Then he replied simply: "OK with me."

The newspaper's promotion department wanted a picture of Vukovich in the winning car, with several children in his lap and a few puppies crammed in, too. When the youngsters and puppies were piled on, "he perked up," as the reporter described it, "and his eyes lit up like Christmas tree ornaments. I never forgot it. I got the idea that kids and dogs he trusted — the average adult, he wasn't so sure."

The reporter wrote the story and Bill did not ask to see it before it was printed. It read:

"I'm not much of a race driver. But when I can't go 500 miles I'll quit. They say you can't start from that far back … and win. But we showed them. This race wasn't much different from others.

"I figured we were winning toward the end of the race. You never can tell early because everybody is going like hell. Besides, you never can tell when one of these things is going to quit. You just run till they blow up.

"How did I feel during the race? Not much of anything. The heat didn't bother me. I didn't worry about the speed, either. And I never think about that northeast curve.

"The race is going to get faster. Every year they say they can't go any faster, but they do.

"I hear they're saying that maybe the caution light helped me win toward the end. That's a bunch of bull. I'll admit I'm not much of a race driver, but I've got a helluva lot of company."

The story took some wheedling and some strain and some leading questions, but enough of Vukovich came through to reveal once again his self-deprecation, his disdain for phony dramatics, his awareness of detractors — and his willingness for once, perhaps, to "cooperate" (that holy word of conformists) in his press and public relations.

His words were read with much unhappiness in some offices and garages in the racing world; some race officials and reporters groaned at what they thought was slighting regard for their sport by its champion. They envisioned another year of hard going for promoters and program chairmen seeking Vukovich's appearance. They felt once more they'd been deprived of the pliable representative who could speak eloquently of their rough, often-misunderstood sport.

The public? It now seemed to regard Bill as a whole-souled man who did what he wanted to do, said what he wanted to say, and answered the challenge of his hazardous urge completely. Many were convinced nothing could defeat him.

❖

For several days after the race Vukovich asked that the garage doors be kept closed to keep out the curious, especially the newsmen, whose questions he no longer wanted to wrestle. But with his own people he unwound, reminiscing freely. Once he stopped by McGrath's quarters for a chat and told Jack he was going to buy a race car next year. McGrath asked, "Why don't you buy something useful, like a grocery store?" Bill snorted and grinned and, knowing there was no point in it, didn't bother to answer.

The crew did some reminiscing, too, about the race. The others were quick to give Hilborn credit for doping out the pit stops. Straw still felt relief whenever he looked at the nicks on the pressure plate of one of the wheels that had been damaged in the first pit stop. He had been, he admitted, a bit nervous while changing the wheel. "My first two blows," he said, pointing to the plate. "I told myself, 'You dumb jerk!' But I didn't want to break the valve stem." Beckley had to smile, recalling Bill looking over at him and Mel during the actress' kiss. "His eyes were twinkling, and he was really living it up — with Marie down his throat about a yard."

꩜

At the Victory Dinner, Vukovich checked the ceiling again while Shaw called up the drivers to receive their checks, the most lucrative ever signed by Speedway owner Tony Hulman. Bryan, who sat on a foam rubber cushion because of his raw underside, received a second-place prize of $35,885 — the payment Vukovich had said he'd refuse to settle on in advance. When it came Bill's turn, he was handed a bulging manila envelope holding checks for $74,935. Now he had won more money than anyone in Speedway history, a total of $185,037. The official Speedway corporation cash payout itself was $88,862, second to Shaw's $91,300. His lap earnings were now $57,750, almost ridiculously ahead, with Holland next at $30,060. The remainder of the winnings were from accessory companies.

With the reading of the prize list, the picture-taking and the applause all concluded, Vukovich leaned slightly toward the mike and — wishing he were miles away — murmured: "I'd like to thank Tony Hulman and Howard Keck and my two mechanics for making it possible for me to win this thing."

He started to turn away, but Shaw called him back to introduce Travers and Coon. He did and then sat down. Afterwards the crew needled him about the prize money that was about $15,000 less than the previous year: "Hey, Smoky; you won't need as many tin cans to bury in the backyard this year."

10

"The money doesn't interest me. I'll go where I please."

Confronting Change

Bill wanted little to do with racing following his victory. But in those despairing days in May when the Kecks feared they would never get the car to behave, he had agreed to race at Milwaukee in a 100-miler the Sunday after the "500."

He tried to go back on his commitment but faced serious backlash. One self-interested promoter proclaimed Vukovich should be an "active champion."

"What for?" Bill asked. "I won the big one. The money doesn't interest me. I'll go where I please."

Esther, too, didn't want him to race at Milwaukee — grateful for one more day free of worry — but as a driver's wife, of course, she kept her feelings to herself.

The wishes of a lesser light would have been respected, there being an unwritten law in racing that no one pushes a driver into a race for which he doesn't feel comfortable. With all the inherent risks, he is at least granted peace of mind. But the crowd appeal of Vukovich was too big a money-maker to let get away and the Milwaukee promoters complained to the racing division of the American Automobile Association. The latter, notorious for siding with management over drivers, threatened Vukovich with suspension if he didn't appear.

Bill wanted to be eligible for another "500" so at the last minute he flew up to Milwaukee. He stepped into the second place "500" finisher, the Dean Van Lines dirt car that Bryan still wasn't healed enough to drive, and qualified fastest. But the car grew progressively unmanageable in the race. Brawner had adjusted the weight to make it fit for a track that would become oily as the race progressed, but the surface remained unusually dry, and Bill had to wrestle a contrarian car. Others, racing behind him, marveled how Bill held on, but on the seventy-first lap of the scheduled 100 on the asphalt oval, his car holding up traffic, Bill brought it in. He'd given it all he had.

He returned to Indianapolis to get on with the business of doing what he wanted, although forgetting to take along the clock he had won for sitting on the pole in Milwaukee.

He sat in the sun and lounged in the Speedway garage and savored the spiritual nourishment of the victory. In Gasoline Alley only an occasional crunch of gravel underfoot or the soothing hiss of a cleaning spray disturbed the quiet or broke the murmur of low, calm conversation. Mechanics stared at a task a long time before stirring and usually decided to have a cold beer or Coke first. There were no other reporters around. I was now more visitor than newsman.

"Bill," I asked, "If you had $100,000 in the bank now would you race?"

"Hell no."

Several among the audience in the Keck garage greeted Bill's answer derisively.

Bill ignored them and went on.

"I figure I'm the most fortunate guy that ever came to this track. I got here in '51 and a guy gives me a ride and a driver's test. Then we were same as third money in '52. Then two firsts.

"That was the most exciting time I had — in '52. No one figures us to be leading that race. In '53 everybody says, 'You should win this one; you're gonna win.' Figure it's coming to you. Hell, they took all the joy out of it, like you're supposed to sit down at dinner at 5 o'clock."

"What about this year; was it exciting?"

"Hell, after a while it gets like eating hamburger." He stopped and grinned. "I felt pretty good at about 100 miles."

His train of thought jumped a few rails. "Everybody calls me a sonuvabitch but there's one thing they can't say about me: I never conned anybody in my life."

Travers, who watched zealously over Keck's generous money, interjected: "What Howard wants is to have something newer and better than the next guy. But he doesn't ever brag about it. He just gets a personal thrill out of it. He says, 'If I ever get mad in this racing business I'll get out. It's supposed to be relaxation for me.'"

Travers went on to say that they hadn't really made money, even in winning, because Keck had spent so much going "first cabin."

"What's it take to run here, Bill?" I asked.

"It doesn't take a big, muscular guy. It takes somebody who can relax. To run this race, you've got to go hard all day. Those guys up front — McGrath, Bryan and Daywalt — I knew they were flying. I wasn't kidding myself. They were running better than we were. Travers and the guys knew that, too; but you gotta go hard all day. I knew that.

"You can't crow. A guy doesn't have to brag about what he's done or what he can do. People know that. They find that out. Guys were saying, 'You can't win two in a row.' I didn't say nothing and just let them talk. But I knew Rose and Shaw won two in a row — and they weren't supermen. A guy can keep on winning here. He's gotta have luck, sure, and the right combination; but it's not impossible. Nothing's impossible!"

He clipped off the last two words, half angry.

I asked Bill if he was superstitious. I knew his attitude about it and the usual racetrack superstitions: avoiding the color green, not eating peanuts in the pits, no picture-taking just before a race — but I wanted to hear it from him.

"Hell, what's superstition?" he said. "We race for green money."

"How long you going to race here?"

"There's no use guessing when you don't know."

The passenger car world was not going to let Bill go home to Fresno without playing its siren song on a cash register, and increasing the volume when he resisted it. Chrysler had just completed a new proving ground at Chelsea, Mich. that it wanted to publicize in dramatic fashion. Its idea: have the top four "500" finishers race, one at a time, against the clock on its 4.7-mile concrete oval. McGrath, Bryan, Ruttman and Vukovich were invited. Bill was offered $2,500. He declined. Not until the pitch rose to $5,000, with Travers the go-between, did Bill assent.

After that he returned to Indianapolis, gathered up his money and other prizes from the "500" — the convertible pace car, a one-year free meal ticket, a cocker spaniel puppy, a case of dog food, a traveling bag, a ring, a 57-piece tool set, a wristwatch and three trophies — and went home to Fresno.

→-←

Through the summer the invitations to show himself in a race car kept coming, gold-coated, one a $2,500 guarantee for a single race, another a $1,000 per week offer from an automobile thrill show. He ignored them. Instead, he bought two service stations and a lot on which someday he hoped to build a new home. The money left over went into the trust fund.

Six days a week, from 8:30 a.m. to 5:30 p.m., he worked at the smaller station near downtown Fresno — pumping gas, wiping windshields, working the grease rack, cleaning out the restrooms — thus making unique the experience of his customers, who had no less a person servicing their cars than the leading figure in the automotive racing world.

Fresno's citizens, from the mayor who watched him drive to work each day, to the kid whose jalopy was on the lubrication hoist, got a kick out of seeing him hustle about in his grease monkey's garb. He took time out only for a coffee break. Any of his friends who wanted an early cup with him had to arise at dawn when he did.

Various promoters and AAA members regarded him as an ingrate who was "not doing anything for racing." Being a solid citizen, uninterested in selling his name, apparently wasn't enough. Bill, meanwhile, went on counting the pennies — the steady pennies — from the gasoline station and fretted over the fractions of profit.

Racing wasn't out of his thoughts by any means. He was now faced, as a matter of fact, with his most vital decision since first he made up his mind to try Indianapolis. What about the car?

The Keck group was at a crossroads. All four — Keck, Vukovich, Travers and Coon — knew those who stand pat seldom win at the Speedway. New ideas, new equipment are necessary. Just how much should they change? It is not often that a new car wins at Indianapolis. Some bugs can be discovered only in the crucible of the 500 miles, making the first race something of a shakedown cruise. But less often does a tired automobile win. In a large sense the Indianapolis Speedway car is a Roman candle flashing through space and expiring with suddenness. The gallant Fuel Injection Special was three years old now.

Keck decided temporarily to try something new, so he set Travers and Coon to work in Los Angeles directing design and construction of a streamliner with a supercharged V-8 engine. Bill, firmly believing the little car had run its course, wanted to retire it. But Travers and Coon, though proceeding with the new project, thought there still might be more left in the enduring gray machine. They were aware, perhaps, they were being ruled by sentiment, but they did not want to give up on the champ, at least until it had been beaten.

And so late in September 1954 the three of them — Vukovich, Travers and Coon — quietly returned to the Speedway track to see how much machine they had left. On the fifth day there, the three of them almost swallowed up in the deserted, gigantic grounds, Bill worked the car up to 137 mph. After he brought it back, they discovered that the crankcase was cracked. Shades of May, and worse. If the car's transmission had locked as a result during the run, Bill might have been hurt. There was nothing to do now but to take the car back, their mission unaccomplished. Bill, already believing the car didn't have it anymore, now had what he thought was the clinching argument.

Even though the defect was freakish and the case could be replaced, the consideration that weighed heaviest on their minds was Bill's reluctance. It is all but axiomatic that no matter how superior the equipment underneath the chauffeur, if he doesn't have confidence in it, success will not come. Travers knew that and did not push Bill to continue with the old car.

⤞⤝

That evening Bill stopped in at the Turf Bar near the Speedway, where several members of the racing fraternity in town for the Hoosier Hundred, a dirt track event at the state fairgrounds, had gathered. It turned quickly into a session needling Bill. When the subject got around to the roadsters now invading the "500" and their smooth riding characteristics, Bill drew a laugh when he remarked, "Hell, some of these new roadsters don't even give you a bump. I don't think the guys got tired; they just fell asleep."

He went on, giving his philosophy on racing. Mechanic George Salih spoke an aside to one of the listeners: "He's got a mind of his own and he uses it." But Emil Andres, a retired driver, touched by the humanness of this man who ruled their world, addressed him directly: "Hell, Vuk, some guys win this thing and then you can't talk to them; look at you sitting here …"

A few seconds of silence followed. The only one showing embarrassment over the compliment, however, was Bill, whose humble reaction only made the others feel warmer toward him.

Before he left Indianapolis, he suggested we get together for a farewell cup of coffee. He talked with clipped intensity, leaning forward, then settling back in the booth. I listened and asked only an occasional question. The next "500" was more than several months away, but it sat heavily on his mind.

"You know who won that race this year?" Bill asked. "Stu Hilborn. You know, there's a smart sonuvabitch. He's a slide-rule guy. He figured out our tire wear and figured that we could go the rest of the way on them and when I came in the second time, he told the guys to fill the tank up because I could go all the way on the tires … I didn't have to come in for more gas and Firestone said I had fifteen more hard laps on those tires."

"What about Vukovich's winning the race?"

He didn't answer, instead looking away. Then he went on:

"You know, after I won in '53 Keck got me aside and told me to be a humble guy, not to let my head get big. Crap, why does a guy have to change? A guy would have to start leading a new life if he's going to try to be somebody he isn't. The hell with them. I know there are a lot of good chauffeurs in this thing. It takes a good combination. A lot of guys don't know it, but the pit crew is a damned important thing. In '52 when we wuz running all the guys leading came in about the same lap. We had damned good pit stops and I was out of there while other guys were fouling up in the pits and killing engines. You know, around here if you lose some time, you never make it up. You've had it.

"I was really sloppy in this race, all over the track, but I kept waving to the 3-A guys, figuring they'd say, 'Hell, he isn't in trouble if he can wave.'"

I tried once more to lure Bill into giving himself credit. "If all the equipment is the same anymore around here, isn't the chauffeur more important than ever?"

"Yes," Bill replied reluctantly. But that's all he would give himself, and he jumped to something else. "When you go looking for trouble you can find it. I keep my mouth shut around here and learn a lot. Sometimes I tell a guy I know something when I don't, just to get him started on something. But when I've got something to say to a guy, I say it.

"You know, some guys win this thing and then they drive right by your house. They used to have coffee with you. Then when they start going down the gutter, they start talking to you again.

"Everyone wants the 'hot dog.' But I've been around, too."

Then, the problem of the uncertain car came to the fore: "I got no kick coming from Howard Keck. He's treated me all right. I don't think Howard wants to run next year with this car. You've got to progress around here. This car is the same it's been for three years. I'm not kidding, I drove as hard as I could this year. That sonuvabitch wasn't running. I'm not saying this to bullshit anybody, but a lot of guys wouldn't have been running it. But I knew if I brought it in a lot of guys would have been happy, so I said to hell with them. It was pushing, the front end drifting all the time — I couldn't pass anyone this year. I'd take Hanks into the turns, and he'd blow me off coming onto the chutes."

I asked about finances and contracts next. "I drive for 40 percent," Bill said. "Some guys want the guy they drive for to put them on salary or to advance them some money. Hell, no one ever paid me a nickel before I drove. Ain't that crude, to ask a guy to advance you some dough? Hell, I wouldn't have the crust to ask a guy like that. They'll give you what's coming to you."

His dark eyes flashed, and his back was up. "Only in '52 I signed. Hell, from then on just our word."

I recalled what Beckley had said once: "Vukovich spoils an owner; he doesn't ask for a nickel."

I asked if he had kept newspaper clippings, watches, trophies and other prizes.

"Hell, I was stupid. Maybe I'll snip something here or there. But the stuff is thrown in some corner. You get tired of the stuff. But I've got some I want to keep. I gave Howard (Keck) the watch I got for sitting on the pole in '53. I thought he'd get a kick out of it … I've got a beautiful trophy for a race I won at Gilmore. I got a bigger kick out of winning it than I did at Indianapolis. I'm not kidding."

"Why?"

"I don't know. Gilmore was a helluva nice guy and that was a swell racetrack."

"I understand you're planning a new home."

"Yeh, I'm going to build a house. You know, kids get big, and you got to have more room. They were selling lots around there for $3,000 and here was this guy who had to sell right away, and I told him I'd give him $1,600 cash right now. He'd seen my picture and knew who I was."

His tone implied shame; he was berating himself for using his fame as a bargaining lever. He waited a moment before continuing: "It's real nice around there; one of the finest schools in the country is nearby."

Eventually Bill guided the conversation back to racing. "I like to drive out in front by myself. Some guys say they like to ride behind a guy, but not me. You know when you get hurt? Some guy in front loops or gets into trouble and you get it, too."

We rose, arguing as always over the check. Neither of us knew a prophecy had just been made.

He had something to do before going back to California, though. Elisian had been badly hurt in a sprint car race in Ft. Wayne, Ind. His right arm and shoulder were severely mauled when he overturned in a collision. Bill bought Ed a plane ticket to Oakland, his home, to use upon his release from the hospital and presented it to him. Then he drove Ed's passenger car to Oakland.

11

"He still has his hungry shoes on."

At the Crossroads

At this point in his career Vukovich had interest in just one race away from Indianapolis: The Mexican Road Race in November. That wild, bloody 2,000-mile contest through tortuous, windy mountains and placid plains still challenged him, even though the stock car was not his medium. He accepted Lincoln's offer again.

Just before leaving Fresno, in a quiet conversation in the living room, he matter-of-factly told Esther, "I have a feeling I'm going to get on my head down there." Esther was taken by surprise — this was the closest thing to fear she had ever heard.

"Why are you going, then?"

"I promised I would."

Nearly a month of dry runs preceded the race. His co-pilot and navigator, Vern Houle, like other co-drivers, marked each turn, its direction, and the fastest possible safe speed with which it could be taken.

Three days before the race the phone rang in the Vukovich house. Esther picked it up. It was Bill.

"Where are you?" she asked.

"I'm at International Airport in Los Angeles. Come up and get me."

'What are you doing there? You're supposed to be in Mexico."

"I know it. But I wanted to come home. I don't like it down there."

Homesickness had proved too much for him. The Lincoln team manager, Bill Stroppe, had told him he couldn't go back, the race was just a couple of days off. Bill answered by taking the first plane out of Mexico.

So, he spent a happy day-and-a-half with his family, then flew back to Tuxtla, the starting point at the bottom of Mexico, only hours before the dawn beginning of the race.

The Mexicans had regarded Bill as the "Crazy Russian." But that night in Tuxtla there was a Soap Box Derby-type race for youngsters. Bill drifted into the crowd, composed mostly of peasants, to watch the kids prepare their cars. He noticed one boy having trouble with his machine. With time short, the lad became frantic and dissolved in tears. Bill saw the chain linkage of the car had fouled and the youngster would not be able to move.

He rushed to the Lincoln team garage, grabbed tools, ran back, lifted the boy out of the car, turned it over, furiously fixed the gear chain and reinserted the lad into the cockpit, in time. Quickly, without ever having said a word to anyone, he disappeared into the crowd. The peasants had watched him silently, absorbing the scene. From that moment on he was no longer the "Crazy Russian." Native grapevine relayed the story with the speed of the wind through the countryside and the Mexicans took Bill for their own.

In the race, Vukovich drove crazy, always past the speed his co-pilot Houle had mapped. Horrified, Houle protested again and again. Bill finally got the leader, Ray Crawford, in sight. They were in the mountains, on a narrow, winding road. They careened around a tight curve, and Bill lost control. He deliberately spun the car, hoping to keep it from going over the embankment. They skidded 150 yards, left the road, rolled over, and plunged down a fifty-foot cliff. As they tumbled, Bill kept asking Houle if he was all right. Then in mid-air, seconds from possible death, he blithely chirped to Vern: "Well, you've been wanting to drive this thing; you've got it now."

The door was ripped off Houle's side. When they came to a stop he looked out. They were teetering on the break of another drop, this one thirty feet.

Miraculously Houle suffered only a bruised arm. Bill, however, had a cracked neck vertebra. The intense pain in his neck was magnified by his sorrow over failing to earn money for Houle.

He refused medical attention although the injury had so nearly paralyzed him that he had to ask Stroppe to lift his legs over the short ledge of the shower stall that evening. When he was dressed, he informed Stroppe and the doctors Stroppe had anxiously called that he was going home. All pleaded with him to have the neck put in traction. Their arguments fell on stubborn ears. He was going home.

Finally, one of the doctors declared strongly: "We refuse to let you go unless we at least plaster a collar on your neck to immobilize it. You have a nerve pinched in such a way that a wrong turn of your head and you will be paralyzed for life."

"Okay, put the damn collar on," Bill said. Groggy from sedatives, he climbed aboard a plane, alone. En route to Los Angeles he became so sickened by the pain and discomfort that he fainted. Passengers — strangers — rushed to his aid and revived him. He let them order a stretcher for him at the airport, where they had landed in a thick fog. An ambulance hustled him to Cedars of Lebanon Hospital.

Once more Esther answered the telephone and heard Bill's voice coming from an unexpected place. He told her he was in a hospital but omitted the details of his collapse. He added that because of the fog he didn't think he could get home that night.

Esther started out with a friend at 7 the next morning, but the fog had hung throughout central and southern California, and they were forced to drive slowly. They didn't arrive until noon.

Bill was on wobbly feet when they reached his room, trying to put on his shoes, preparing to leave. His first words were a bark: "Where you been?!"

A harassed nurse standing near turned toward Esther, happy to have some help. "He's checked out three times!" she said.

They drove him home, but Bill had to lie down in the back seat to lessen the pain. For the next six weeks Esther handled the driving because Bill's neck injury prevented him from even being able to push the brake pedal.

The confinement grew intolerable, and he sneaked out of the house occasionally to drive away. But he'd return in fifteen minutes because of the pain. Finally, the doctor, knowing of the "escapes," leveled with him: "That vertebra up there is connected to your spine, Bill." The tone was sobering. For the first time he capitulated completely. He wanted to be ready for Indianapolis, so he kept himself still and in the house. When his $3,000 guarantee for the Mexican Race arrived from the Lincoln people, he gave half of it to Houle. It was his way of apologizing.

When he was well enough again, he returned to the service station routine and continued making plans for the new house. He attended the *Los Angeles Times* "champions" dinner this time, with his family, gave a short and embarrassed "thank you" at the rostrum and virtually ran back to the table to rejoin Esther and the kids.

He made excuses to avoid other public appearances, but he accepted a local high school's invitation to look at an auto engine that was part of their training and he liked going to the Veterans Hospital to offer commentary on a film of the "500" for the patients.

Stroppe asked him to attend a large press party in Long Beach honoring the Lincoln team, which had dominated the Mexican Road Race. He arrived late, protested putting on "that damned monkey suit," held still for two pictures, sneaked back into the office, folded the driving uniform, laid it on a chair and disappeared.

Promoters had given up on him, but he was still sought for testimonials. He disliked that business, too. He turned down all but three endorsements — two auto accessories and one food product. Having always had to struggle for his money, he never quite accepted the idea that merely signing his name was honest enough effort to receive compensation.

He also permitted one other tiny crack in his armor against the conventions of society. He became a joiner for the first and only time. The Elks in Fresno sought him, and he accepted their invitation.

✦

Meanwhile, Travers and Coon continued working on the new Keck car. By winter, however, they resigned themselves to the reality it couldn't be ready for the 1955 race. They knew repairing the cracked crank case would be simple, but the Fuel Injection had become too risky to race again. Bill was reluctant to stay with the old car, anyway, and Keck had all but decided not to enter the '55 race. They all had to start shopping among the car owners.

One owner guaranteed Bill $7,000. Another offered him 70 percent of the earnings. Both were fantastic offers. But he turned both down. He didn't think either car was capable of winning.

Travers, Coon and Vukovich learned via the grapevine — an active, well-nourished medium in auto racing — that owner Lindsey Hopkins and driver Pat O'Connor might not be teamed again. Hopkins, a veteran sportsman prominent on the Indianapolis scene, was in Atlanta attending to the money-making — real estate, primarily. Multi-cornered communications began. Vukovich sought out Henry Banks, a close friend of Hopkins, about the possibility of racing for the latter. Banks and Hopkins were elated that the champ was interested. The telephone wire between Atlanta and Fresno began humming.

Bill stated his position:

"Listen, Lindsey, I'm not trying to shoot anyone out of the saddle. If O'Connor is still the driver of the car, he's going to drive it. I just want you to know that if O'Connor isn't going to drive for you, I'm available."

Lindsey assured Bill the split with Pat was amicable and the seat was open. Hopkins called Keck to tell him he would not sign Bill without Keck's permission. Keck gave it to him.

The negotiations were brief and non-haggling, remarkable considering the talent and money involved between Vukovich and Hopkins. Bill wanted his beloved Beckley "butchers" — Travers and Coon — to come with him. Hopkins, aware he was striking it rich, gladly agreed. Bill would drive for 40 percent of the earnings. Undoubtedly, he could have received 50 percent considering his reputation and his delivery of the winning mechanics. The alert Hopkins knew what he had going for him now.

Esther asked Bill why he had stopped at 40 percent.

"I could have held the guy up, I guess, but I didn't want to," he said. "I probably could have got $2,000 more like other guys would have.

Sure, I can use $2,000. Who can't? But I wanted to show Lindsey what I could do."

Winter turned to spring and Bill stepped up his training routine — miles of road work, more miles on the bike, and more calisthenics. He indulged only in an infrequent beer or a mild cigar. He spent virtually every evening at home with the family. His arm around Esther, he would remark happily: "What would I be doing now if I was single?" Occasionally, friends came over to play cards.

The major national magazines seemed finally to have heard of him. Two called on him. They extracted few quotes from him directly, for they had approached a difficult man in a difficult sport to write about. One article was titled, "The Grape Picker and the 500 Miles," profiling him as "a Grapes of Wrath" character. It contained inaccuracies but also offered a highly accurate characterization. The other article emerged later: "Why Vukovich Has to Win the 500." Its premise was highly debatable.

As spring arrived and the racing season resumed, some of the people nearest to Bill began to grow anxious. Must he risk his life another time? A third victory at Indianapolis would only add statistical distinction. He had already carved an indelible niche.

"Why don't you retire?" Faulkner asked.

"I'll quit as soon as I can't get the job done," Bill replied.

Henrietta Motter thought: "Billy is changed. It isn't the money because he's made it. Maybe it's because people keep pushing him and expecting him to race again at Indianapolis and win again."

Earl Motter wondered, too: "He isn't fighting for pennies anymore."

Esther thought her husband needed to prove something to himself.

As was his pre-departure custom, Vukovich warmed up with some midget competitions. At Gardena he raced for nickels but, faithful to his instinct and his belief that the people who bothered to come deserved his best, he deliberately nudged Jimmy Reece out of the way to win. The fans, amazed, stood and cheered. The public address man said simply, "Ladies and gentlemen, that was the Indianapolis champion." In the pits one man observed: "He still has his hungry shoes on."

But at Phoenix a tow truck inexplicably crossed the track in front of him and he crashed into it. He inherited an enormous bruise near a shin bone, which he ignored until it began to fester.

Two weeks before Bill was to leave for Indianapolis, Esther had a dream, the first one about racing she'd ever had. In it there was a race car — not necessarily Bill's — that had just flipped and was lying flat, a cloud of dust rising from it. At breakfast she related it to Bill. He dismissed it lightly.

"Aw, forget it. That's nothing."

Just before he left, Henrietta Motter said quietly to Earl: "He's going to be killed at Indianapolis this year."

"If you turn right, then you're in trouble."

Back to Indianapolis

Bill had grown up with Motter, celebrated with him when Billy and Marlene were born, and shared with him what few confidences he dared reveal. Faulkner had been a fellow Depression kid and had survived the early racing jungle with him, risking their necks, as Walt phrased it, "for burnt matches and peanut shells." Elisian had become his adopted racing son.

En route, the three absorbed the typical Vukovich idiosyncrasies, such as the impatient stops where he harangued them because they weren't eating quickly enough. Bill's kid sister, Florence, in similar circumstances used to order small meals to keep up with him, and when once he asked her if she didn't have enough money to eat more, she didn't have the heart to tell him why. Despite sharing the ride with three other professional racers, he drove all but fifty miles of the way.

At times Faulkner thought Bill had something on his mind, that the Vukovich spark was dampened. He wondered if Bill was depressed because he felt he had to win three in a row, because people had built him up so.

The conversation in the car was lively. Once, when the topic was automobile accidents, one of them mentioned a crash in which a man was burned to death.

Vukovich hunched his shoulders in imitation of a sudden chill, and shuddered: "Boy, what an awful way to die."

That comment brought to Earl's mind another remark Bill had once made to him: "Someday, they'll have to pick me up off a racetrack." He had not said it fearfully. He'd gone on to add that the only thing he'd hate to have happen to him would be to burn to death.

Upon arriving in Indianapolis Bill went straight to the Speedway rather than checking in at the Thompsons. He was met at the garage gate by reporters with pencils at the ready. As the two-time defending champion, he was hot copy. He reacted to them a little less warily than before, a bit more relaxed.

Nearly every driver's arrival is an occasion for a bull session. The more highly-rated the driver, the bigger the boasting about what he'll do this year. Each man's psychological war starts then. Though Bill could pour it on with the best of them he disguised his true feelings.

Consequently, each listener was left to his own interpretation when Bill declared, upon questioning by reporters: "Sure I'm going to win. I didn't come back here for my health … There are two ways to win this race. If you can't outrun 'em, outlast 'em."

He was grinning as he talked and squeezing a hand exerciser. He acknowledged that, sure, he was in a different car this time but didn't think it would matter.

"It doesn't make any difference what you win in. You can win this thing … I'm gonna blow 'em all off. All these cars turn left. If you turn right, then you're in trouble."

Upon reaching the safe cocoon of his garage, he squared his shoulders and looked out the door in a happy mood. "I never felt better and had less. Ho! Ho!" He looked and sounded fit.

As he whiled away the time waiting for Travers and Coon to roll in with the car, he talked about his service stations — "I was working in the damn place like a coolie, like I hadn't eaten for 10 years," — and about his public relations — "I'm still insulting people and I'm still getting free meals." That statement was less a commentary on himself than on name droppers and hero worshippers.

Very late in the day tired-eyed travelers Travers and Coon completed their journey from the West Coast with the bright blue Hopkins Special. It was a later model Kurtis Kraft — only two years old — that was wider but lighter and more rigid than their previous car. As the reception party gathered in the garage, Bettenhausen made a remark about the tail. Bill shot back, fiercely:

"Don't be looking at the tail. You'll be seeing it May 30th. Look at the front now while you have a chance."

Everyone turned to look at Vukovich, who now was grinning.

With the unloading and garage cleanup completed and the reception party gone, Travers lamented the fates that prevented completion of the new Keck car that Howard had wanted to run again. The three reminisced for a while about faithful little No. 14, but Bill suddenly cut it off.

"It's too late now. We'll do the best we can."

Bill picked up a rag and wiped the travel dust from the cockpit. Then he stood looking at it for a long, long time.

That first night he visited with friends until 3 in the morning. He didn't want to awaken the Thompsons at that hour, so he slept in his passenger car.

That first week of May, while Travers and Coon readied the car for the initial warmup on the racetrack, Vukovich confined himself almost exclusively to his garage — No. 7 this time, a few doors from his old home, No. 11. At times he unburdened himself. Magazine stories were appearing on the stands by now, but as with all the newspaper stories written in recent years, he claimed not to have read them.

Under questioning, though, he revealed annoyance at a couple of points — and thus belied the lack of interest he'd always professed about what was written about him. Proudly, he denied what he called "that Grapes-of-Wrath crap" that was a popular theme in stories about him.

"My father raised eight kids but there was plenty of grub," he said. "We had bicycles and a Shetland pony."

But the reminder of his austere background struck a chord. "Nothing's hard to do if you really want to do it," he said. "Everybody sits around feeling sorry for himself and bleeding. Just put your mind to something."

His thoughts projected into the future, too: "A guy can make a living without racing. I've got some things I want to do after the race. I've been thinking about a car wash and a drive-in restaurant. I get tired of hanging around race drivers. The same old yak-yak for fifteen years. A guy ought to do something else. Esther wants me to build a new house. You know, that's what a guy should get out of life, a nice home."

The urge to get into a cockpit was so great that late on his fifth day at the Speedway he borrowed McGrath's car. He put on his helmet in the same business-like manner as he did on race day. A bystander asked Jack if he was hoping some of Vukovich would rub off on the car. McGrath smiled and said if that were possible, then Bill could drive it all day.

Bill took it up only to 128 mph. When he was asked, tongue-in-cheek, if he was planning to be a co-pilot, he countered seriously: "When the day comes I can't do it alone, I'll quit."

He took the Hopkins car out for the first time the next day, but only briefly, then took several laps the following day, reaching 135 twice. Travers waved at him to return to the pits five times, starting with a casual looping of his left arm, then more urgently and pointedly. Before Travers finally got his message across, pit wags were suggesting lassoes.

"It would be kinda nice to see if anything's about to fall off the thing," Travers muttered with a trace of annoyance. Coon, his usual imperturbable self, casually suggested limiting the fuel the next time out.

On May 9th, McGrath threw down the gauntlet. The practice day was unfavorably cold and windy, but Jack found it monotonous sitting around all weekend in the same conditions.

"We decided even though it was blowing to say, 'to hell with it,' and go," he said.

When he drove the first lap in the Hinkle Special with obvious speed, stop watches blossomed like dandelions. The unofficial watches caught McGrath in four laps at better than 140 mph, with a 141.066 trip the best. The official standards of 141.287 (one lap) and 141.033 (four laps), set by McGrath the previous year, appeared doomed.

The clickety-click of Bill's hand-grippers became a familiar sound in the garage area. He squeezed them closed as if they were no more resistant than a pair of pliers. Occasionally he'd offer them to an unsuspecting bystander to test his grip. That person would be fortunate to manage a dozen compressions. Bill went to 100 rapidly. When the crew left a wheel jack standing on end at the doorway of the garage he reached up to the cross bar and chinned himself swiftly a dozen times.

He kept up the psychological warfare, too. "I'm going to get Howard to buy the Speedway, so I can invite all the people I like to beat." Or, "If I'd known how easy it was here I'd have brought along my grandmother to run second." Or, "Racing is a hobby; I work for a living."

But he wasn't as visible at the track as previous years. He spent considerably more time at the Thompson home than in previous Mays. He chatted at length with Dorcas Thompson, showing unusual interest in her life. He asked about her daughter, Susie, who was Marlene's age and often exclaimed, "Oh, she does that, too? I wondered, because that's what Marlene does." Dorcas smiled at his innocence regarding his children.

The lure of the track was not as strong as before, and he spent more time in the house watching television and listening to the radio. He told Dorcas, "I've got a radio going here and I can hear the cars going by. Why do I want to go over there and waste my time watching?"

Soon thereafter, however, he would walk over to the track.

The atmosphere at the Speedway seemed out of joint at times. The weather, for one, was weird — cold, windy, cloudy, and often rainy. Freak mishaps were occurring on the track, too. There was a spinout that resulted when an unobservant driver, Leroy Warriner, raced through at least four yellow lights and some hand signals to come onto a scene of a wall-smashed car and attending fire truck. His car suffered only minor damage, but he was fined $50 and lost the seat in the car. There were an unusually heavy number of drivers racing one another in practice, which was exasperating to the mechanics who were more interested in testing. In the final hours of practice before the first qualification day, there were three spins, one wrecked car and a second one damaged.

Several drivers had reached practice speeds of 140 mph, but not Bill. So, he, Travers and Coon were not getting much attention.

New year, new car, same crew. (IMS Photos)

However, no one completely ignored Vukovich when he took to the track no matter the troubles they were having with a new car. They had made changes to the gear ratio and the chassis weight distribution but weren't sure if they had helped. Stopwatches always came out for Bill Vukovich, however, and so one day when he came back into view off the fourth turn much sooner than expected, the people on the pit wall became excited. They started their watches. When he returned again, they stared at the clock faces incredulously. Up at the pit apron Travers permitted himself a trace of a grin as he walked over to Hopkins, who also was smiling.

"Time 1:03.8. Speed 141.066."

That was enough. Travers started running south down the pit area to an open spot where he could wave to Bill to bring it in.

The news buzzed through the pit area, infecting all.

Seeing his speeds, Bill said, "Gee, that's good," and almost permitted himself a smile.

Travers said to Hopkins, "Boss, let's get this thing into the barn." Vukovich grabbed the battery cart and soberly pulled it through an aisleway of admiring grinners.

"Well, we're running," he said back in the garage as he patted the car. "It's lovely.

"That little change we talked about did it," he added quietly, turning toward Travers and Coon.

The defending champ had charged back into the "500" picture. If anyone was going to steal the show, they still had to contend with him.

The revitalized Vukovich was on display downtown that evening at the L. Strauss & Co. dinner party, at which his prize for last year's victory, an unfinished portrait of him and his race car, was presented. He was relaxed enough during the meal to put everyone at ease, and he met everyone's verbal challenges head-on and with humor.

The day's successful run had helped him relax. "Those guys thought they were going at 140, didn't they?" he whispered to me at one point. "I kinda cooled 'em off, didn't I?"

To the remainder of the table, informally, he explained: "We weren't running very easy at 139 and I told the guys what was wrong. The gear was too high. You can't run fast with that high a gear. We ran easier at 141 than we did 139." He paused and grinned to deliver a conclusion: "I guess I'm an engineer."

When he was asked if his crew was using nitro, he gave his answer to Speedway owner Tony Hulman: "So help me, Tony, we're not using 'pop.' If you can find any 'pop' in it, I'll give you the car — and it doesn't belong to me."

Someone else wanted to know about the speeds; shouldn't something be done to bring them down to make the race safer? Bill offered a whimsical suggestion: "If you had a two-seater, you could put an owner or a mechanic in it and ask them if they thought you were going fast enough. That would be one way to slow the speeds down."

Speaking to an audience was still something else, however, and he swallowed hard before saying: "I'd like to thank Mr. Hulman and all the people who made it possible for me to win this wonderful painting. Thank you." He was back in his chair before the television news cameraman could get his lens trained on him.

Esther soon arrived in Speedway and filled him in on the goings-on back home, and Marlene and Billy. Just before leaving Fresno, she told him, she had discovered a note on the telephone pad: "Daddy is going to win the 500-Mile Race." And beneath it, in different handwriting: "He always does."

13

"I'll be glad when this rat race is over."

Month of Mishaps

On the first day of qualifications, a Saturday, there came a hard wind, with gusts of up to 40 mph. They were too strong for both the safety and speed of the drivers, so while 75,000 spectators waited, ready crews eyed each other warily, hour after hour.

The feeling at first was that even if a crew ventured out and took the pole, the speed probably would be wiped out if the wind abated later in the day. As the afternoon wore on and the conditions failed to improve, nobody took to the track. Finally, a gentlemen's agreement was reached among the crew members and drivers in contention for pole position not to make an attempt.

McGrath had his car rolled back into the garage, though others who were in on the agreement left their cars near the apron. Bettenhausen eagerly supported the pact. Pat O'Connor agreed only reluctantly. Travers and Coon said they'd go along if that were the desire of the majority. Bill wasn't around when they agreed and when they informed him, he reacted bitterly — but said he would go along with it.

As the remaining time for qualification attempts shrank into minutes crews grew more nervous, knowing there would be a stampede for the pit apron the instant anyone made a move. Vukovich, still believing it should be every man for himself, wanted to return the car to his pit. O'Connor also gave signs of wanting to bolt, and the agreement leaders talked earnestly to him.

Speedway owner Tony Hulman congratulates Vukovich after his record-setting qualification run. Jack McGrath later broke it with a nitro-boosted effort. (Bob Gates collection)

That group had neglected to include everyone in the pact, however. They believed only the realistic pole contenders were needed to make it effective. So, young Jerry Hoyt, lightly regarded, had his car rolled out twenty-seven minutes before the deadline, unaware of any deal having been made. He was quickly apprised of it, but said it was too late to turn back. Fighting the wind, he came back with a 140.045 mph average — and the pole.

The bond had been broken, and as Hoyt's car was wheeled out a small panic ensued as crews lunged at their inert autos, racing against time. Bettenhausen got into line next, and the cars of O'Connor and Hanks almost collided in the rush to join him. Bettenhausen made it out in time and gained second spot in the field, at 139.985. O'Connor got onto the track just before the gun, but his crew didn't consider his 138 average for the first two laps adequate and recalled him.

Waiting futilely behind him were Vukovich, Bob Sweikert and McGrath. Hanks' engine was running when the final seconds before the deadline vanished.

Bill's mood had been jaunty at the start of the day. Full of nervous energy, he was snapping his fingers while he waited and joked with Hopkins. He purposely called him "Howard" and scolded him for borrowing cigarettes. "These owners are always going around bumming cigarettes," he said with feigned exasperation.

"That's the only thing we get free," Lindsey replied in his broad, easy Southern tone.

Bill even found a moment to walk by me and say out of the corner of his mouth, "I didn't like the story you wrote." He kept going, to leave hanging in the air whether he meant it or not. I worried for some time, wondering what could have bothered him about the complimentary article on Thursday's practice breakthrough, then sought him out and offered an apology. Bill winked. "Forget it; us peasants have to take care of each other," he said, and walked away. The door to Vukovich had opened another small crack.

As the intimidating wind continued throughout the day, however, Bill's mood darkened. By late afternoon he was increasingly anxious. "Let's back up the sonuvabitch and if we can get 139-140, let's go," he told his crew before stalking out of the garage.

"Our boy is getting nervous," Travers said.

When the ill-fated "conspiracy," as the disproving element of the sharply divided garage population later described it, fell through because of Hoyt's unknowing betrayal, Vukovich blew up. He blamed Bettenhausen for instigating the idea.

"Crissakes, these guys aren't thinking about you when they make a deal; they're thinking about themselves!" he said. "They're scared … Hell, I told off that Bettenhausen. I told him I'd blow him off. Inside of ten laps he'll be so tired he'll fall out of the seat!

"We should have run! These guys were our friends, huh!"

The crew let him vent. Harley Copp, an urbane Ford Motor Company research engineer and executive whom Bill had met in Mexico and respected, finally brought him down with well-placed shots of banter.

As Bill cooled, his tone softened: "That McGrath was a gentleman, though; he put his car in the garage."

Talking later with Esther, however, he was worked up again. There shouldn't have been an agreement, he railed; the wind didn't matter, the car was okay, he was ready. He had indeed had a terrific argument with Bettenhausen, and he confessed it to Esther and the Thompsons. But now he was miserable about it. At the end of his tirade, subdued, he said, "I've known a lot of people who have disgusted me, but I can honestly say I've never hated anyone."

Dorcas Thompson gave him a long look and thought, *That's quite a statement to make. I know I can't make it.*

⇥⇤

Animosities blew through the Speedway garages the next day, the modest Hoyt unfairly the target of some of it. Jerry sought out Bill to explain his decision to qualify and offer an apology. "Listen, Jerry," Bill said, "if you think what you did was right and you know in your mind it was right, then that's it. Forget it. I'm with you."

Another qualification day was on hand, a fair and hot Sunday. Sweikart, in the John Zink Special dubbed the "Pink Bathtub," was first out, and though his first three laps were 140.165, 139.470, and 139.018, he cut short his trial, the first of the three chances allotted. The general belief in the garage area was that a 139.5 average or better would be needed to make the field. Faulkner was next with a 139.762 and a sigh of relief: "I'm sure as hell glad that's over. Those kids are getting too fast."

Eventually it came Vukovich's turn. He had been nervous waiting in line and didn't settle down until he was in the car. He sat there, awaiting access to the track, oblivious to those around him. One camera recorded a mood that later would be studied and restudied. In full racing dress, helmet on and goggles around neck, he leaned on the left side of the cockpit, resting his elbow, his cheekbone lightly sitting on clenched hand. Eyes half-closed, there was an air of detachment, and his expression could have been interpreted as melancholy, worried, resigned, or poignant. Whatever he felt, he was completely within himself.

He rolled out to the fans' applause, took a slow warmup, raised his hand for the green flag — and evoked a roar of approval with his first lap. It was 141.309 mph, a one-lap record. The next two were identical — 141.066 — and he finished with a four-lap average of 140.845, also a record.

The celebration on his return was relatively quiet, though all the members of his crew laughed when he said, "Sure didn't feel like we were going that fast." Scores of cameras pointed at him. "Hey, Vuky; hey, Vuky!" His smile was partially forced.

His speech over the public address system was, in its entirety, "I'm very happy."

They were taking it in stride now, the "Rich Kids," this continued success. Back in the garage, Bill showed no emotion. "Well, all I care is we're in the race," he said, adding, "This car handles better than the Keck car."

But, he said, "That McGrath is going to go, I'll clue you."

The crew, of course, felt relief over clearing the hurdle into the field of race eligibles, but the joy that usually followed a successful qualifying attempt was difficult to locate.

Elisian, however, raised spirits when he walked into the garage and kidded Vukovich about his qualification run: "Two laps exactly the same. You're finally getting smooth around here. None of this ..." And he went into an exaggerated pantomime of jerky handling of a steering wheel.

Bill had an answer. He held out the card listing his trial speeds and advised Elisian: "Hey, Smoky, put that card on your dashboard when you go out and needle yourself a little."

Two hours, 53 minutes after Vukovich's record was posted McGrath confirmed Bill's belief. Jack buttoned on his jet-pilot helmet, which provided a suitable frame for his gaunt face with its startling white eyebrows, and, in the language of the race crowd, "went like a bomb." His first, almost unbelievable, lap was 143.793. His second, 142.608.

His third, 142.789. And his fourth, 141.454, for an average of 142.580. As onlookers groped for words to describe this lift of the Speedway's ceiling, McGrath provided the most fitting comment himself upon his return: "Most hair-raising ride I ever had. I was scared, I'll guarantee you."

Hopkins, whose car now was only second best, came forward and held out his hand: "Nice going, fella."

And now the photographers were shouting, "Hey, Jack!" "Jack!" "Jack!"

Up at the pit apron, chief Steward Harry McQuinn departed from the AAA's usually sober ways when he picked up the track microphone to advise the unqualified crews with wry recognition of McGrath's terrific achievement: "The track is now open for qualifications and a helluva lot more practice."

Later McGrath elaborated. He had used "pop" — nitromethane — in his engine and had his hands full going into the first turn.

"I wasn't given my time until the third lap and it scared me," he said. "That's the sloppiest four laps I've ever put in here."

He had been a picture of controlled, nervy power, yet he had hurt his performance, he believed, by trying to outthink the wind.

"On the first lap you don't anticipate the wind. But later you try to make allowances and if the wind isn't there when you allow for it you go out into the marbles. I was working at it. I was even sweating."

Before the day was over Bill was third best. Freddie Agabashian, always a fine qualifier, flew around at 141.933, with a high lap of 142.902.

A strange weekend of trials came to an end. There had been a bitter hassle over an arm signal involving Jim Rathmann and the AAA; nineteen attempts that produced only eight successful qualifications; heavy use of the temperamental wonder drug, nitro; and speculation that the slowest speed posted, 139.098, would not stand up. Consistent with that thinking, Manny Ayulo, starting out just two minutes before the qualification deadline, broke off his trial run after laps of 139.470, 138.953, and 139.557.

All the next day — Monday, a practice day — Manny labored over his car. Both mechanic and driver, he was in a hurry to find the extra speed necessary to make the field of thirty-three. Just a few minutes before the track's closing, he ran two laps at a little better than 139 mph. He started a third trip, the last that the 6 p.m. deadline would allow. Most of the few remaining spectators, about to depart, watched him idly as he went by. The bright red car went roaring down the straightaway, came to the end of it, and didn't turn. It went straight into the wall and the horrible impact against the concrete somehow made the car cling to it as it scraped along the curve in a sickening grind for 500 feet.

The grotesquely twisted automobile was still nestled against the wall when the ambulance, reporters, officials, and wrecker pulled up in a fearful pant. The auto's red coat of paint, once conveying aggression, now reflected only alarm. A doctor and emergency crew had to peer down into the cockpit to find Ayulo. He was crumpled deep, beneath the seat, unconscious, bloody, and broken. His face was smashed, right cheekbone bleeding, arms and legs unnaturally twisted, and his barely audible breathing was raspy.

It was later determined he had not been wearing his seat belt. His helmet remained on, but his goggles had shattered, and his shoes had come off. There was a dent in the 14-inch-wide wall and fragments of glass formed a trail along its base.

Helping hands worked carefully and slowly, paying special attention to the excessive bleeding around his mouth. Life seemed to be draining from him in a steady flow of blood and mucus, giving his rescuers a sinking feeling of desperation and sadness.

"Don't let him strangle on his own blood," a mechanic cautioned sharply.

"Now lay him flat on the back of the cockpit," someone else advised.

The doctor, struggling with others to free Manny from under the steering wheel and still not injure him further, murmured, "That's easier said than done." It took several minutes to get him out.

The accident hadn't yet run its course. The right front tire, though it survived the tremendous stress of the impact and scrape, finally yielded and exploded, causing several bystanders to jump.

At the hospital, Manny's jaw and throat were stuffed to stem the bleeding and a tracheotomy was performed to aid his breathing. He had a basal skull fracture, fractured left arm and left leg, injured right arm, broken jaw. He couldn't talk because of the jaw stuffing, but he responded to pain stimulus.

Back at the track the reconstruction of the accident began. There were no skid marks to indicate an attempt by Ayulo to brake out of trouble. He had gone directly into the wall while still hoping, still trying, to turn. The steering wheel was in full throw to the left, but there had been no response. At the last instant the agonized Manny must have braced himself stiff-armed against the steering rim, for he hadn't suffered the chest injury that usually comes with this type of accident.

As the broken car was rolled back to the garage area, curious onlookers swarmed around it. Some women stood at the topmost level of the bleachers, the closest they were permitted to the garages, and looked down on the smashed car, reluctant but not quite repelled. Crews and drivers, the latter swallowing thoughts of "there-but-for-the-grace-of-God-go-I," inspected the wreckage clinically, to see if perhaps there was a lesson to be learned.

The race participants, mechanics and drivers alike, quickly began helping the wrecker crew dismantle the car, as if to erase their memories of the accident and alleviate their anxiety. Wheel lugs, jammed by the crash, resisted. An exceptionally strong man was needed to free them. Jimmy Bryan stepped up, was handed the sledgehammer, and pounded the squealing, protesting lugs loose.

Four doctors ministered to Ayulo through the night and in the morning a special bulletin asking for blood donors was tacked onto the track bulletin board. Steadily as people arrived, volunteers soberly signed their names: Joe Sostillio. Joe Barzda. Jimmy Reece. Bill Vukovich. Barney Christiansen. Jim Byran. Elmer George. Jim Brown. All were drivers but Christiansen and Brown, both mechanics, and Barzda, car owner.

Shortly after noon the list was taken down. Manuel Leaonedas Ayulo, son of a Peruvian diplomat, who had loved autos from childhood, who had a penchant for last-minute thrills for Indianapolis Speedway crowds, who had been straining for another mile per hour of speed, had just died. Unconscious for the nineteen hours since his accident, he'd been overwhelmed by an assortment of injuries. He was 33 years old and had a wife, Charlene, and four-year-old daughter, Frances. At the hospital with Charlene Ayulo, who had not been at the track the day of the accident, were Sam Hanks and Jack McGrath, for whom Ayulo had driven 250 miles of relief four years before to bring McGrath's car to a third-place finish. The Speedway's driver death total was now twenty-five.

The technical committee announced its findings. Vibration had raised and pulled out a bolt and the vertical steering shaft had disengaged from the lower steering arm. A clamp could have kept Ayulo alive.

Word of his death went around the Speedway with the traditional speed of bad news, and it created small knots of people with long faces talking in low voices.

How do those who race cars for a living react after an accident claims the life of one of them? After a while they went about their business. Drivers and crews took cars out to run on the track, for time was short and dwelling on misfortune would not help a man drive up to speeds that can kill. But the usual emotional spark was missing. Mostly, everyone was merely going through the motions.

When the news reached Bryan, he walked over to a passenger car parked in the corner of the garage area, sat in it, and stared out toward the infield of the track. For McGrath, who had begun racing with Ayulo as teammates ten years earlier, the elation of his record-breaking run just two days before was gone. Red-eyed Peter Schmidt, owner of Ayulo's car, was a lost soul trying to collect his feelings. Friends made it a point to approach him and occupy his thoughts.

The Speedway is normally a gagsters' paradise, with ceaseless efforts at humor, much of it succeeding handsomely. Most race drivers have a finely developed wit, a light attitude toward life. This is perhaps nature's compensation to them for the grimness that lies, just a second or an inch — or a clamp — away. But there was no levity this day.

Vukovich had an additional unhappy thought — the bitterness with Bettenhausen, his good friend. Their disagreement gnawed at him. He went up to Tony and announced, "Listen, Bettenhausen. What I said to you I meant, every word of it, at the time. But I don't mean it now."

He'd made his apology honestly, but the residue of their argument still left him feeling guilty, and he asked Esther, "Do you think we ought to go up to Tinley Park sometime?" Tinley Park, Ill. was Bettenhausen's home; it was as if Bill still wanted to make amends by visiting Tony after the race was over.

Most visits, no matter how short, still failed to interest him, however. The Speedway public relations staff met continual resistance from him as clubs in and around Indianapolis sought the champ, or "the hot dog," as Bill phrased it sarcastically. Bob Laycock of the Speedway staff, a large, phlegmatic man, usually inherited the chore of asking Bill. Whenever he saw Laycock approaching he'd either wilt or demand, "What the hell do you want now?"

Told of the appearance request, Bill's first reaction would be to ask if he had to make a speech. Most of the time, though, he wouldn't bother even to do that. He simply gave Laycock a flat "No!"

Anyone less imperturbable than Laycock, whose talent for liaison among the public, the press and racing personnel was of immense value to the Speedway, would have shied from contacting Bill, as indeed the great majority did. But the skirmishes inspired a friendship built on mutual respect. When Vukovich said yes, he made the appearance (aside from the lone exception in Los Angeles) — as opposed to those drivers who pleasantly and obligingly accepted the invitation and then did not show.

When Bill complained, "I don't want to go to those things," Laycock countered, in a soft tone: "You know, Bill, the way to stop all that is to lift your foot a little sooner."

Both enjoyed that remark, knowing *that* concession would never be made.

✦✦

If Vukovich wasn't mixing outside the track he did seem to be fraternizing more often within the Speedway grounds, to the point he was occasionally playing gin rummy in the garage restaurant, favorite haunt of drivers and crews. The conversations there usually began and ended with mention of Vukovich. On one such occasion Bill was playing cards with Andy Linden. The air was full of the champ's name and his deeds when Linden suddenly exclaimed, angrily:

"Vukovich! Vukovich! That's all I hear! Is that Vukovich a god or something?"

The outburst startled the kibitzers around the table. Bill was quick to protest.

"I didn't say anything! I haven't said a word about Vukovich." He hadn't, in fact, but he reacted with a feigned, injured innocence to add fuel to psychological warfare.

But as the card game resumed, he couldn't have been more cordial, lending support to a claim he'd once made to his crew: "These guys think I'm crude. I can be as rough as a cob or as smooth as silk. I can turn on the charm."

The search for speed continued, more frantic as the final week of preparations slipped by. The "safely in" line of prediction now moved up to 140 mph, as driver after driver — even lightly-regarded — turned in at least a 139 practice lap. Forty cars sought the twenty-five unfilled places.

The pace was already at the ragged edge, and the reach for more brought trouble, even calamity.

Paul Russo twice touched the cement wall at 139 mph. He had been blowing by people on the straightaways, and mechanic Herb Porter was beaming. Porter went down to the first turn to see how his painstakingly nursed machine handled itself around a bend. A bearing failed, the impeller fouled, the transmission locked and the once happily whining little car now set up that familiar chilling squeal of a car being braked to avoid disaster. Russo steered frantically, trying to do what frail men can at times like this, and for an instant even thought he would escape the wall, but he backed into it once, spun around and backed in again. Porter watched as every sweating day he'd struggled with the car since the previous June became an exercise in futility.

This is the way of the Speedway — sweat and twist and lift and roll and shove and turn and jack and measure and figure and adjust and increase and decrease and haul and telephone and sit and worry and guess and start and stop and pray and change and exchange; and do it for a year. And then just two days before final qualifications for the big race the beloved, expensive, temperamental metal will behave poorly and all is for naught.

Happily, Russo emerged unscathed. Sympathizers gathered to stare at the car — frame bent, engine askew, front axle gone, damaged beyond two-day repair — as if it were a helpless stricken animal.

Two hours after the blow, which would have devastated lesser men who struggle at the Speedway, the lean, curly-haired Porter remarked sarcastically: "I probably won't try again until next year." A grin played at a corner of his mouth.

The spotlight was avoiding Vukovich these days, what with the urgency involving others and his own frequent absence from the track. But on one visit he said to Elisian, curiously: "You know, Ed, I haven't thought much about winning this race, but I think I'll win it … it isn't very hard." Bill stopped there and Ed, somewhat puzzled, made no attempt to draw him out. Was Bill merely thinking out loud, giving himself a pep talk, trying to ramp up his interest? Elisian didn't know.

Rain threatened as the all-important final weekend of trials arrived. Events of that Saturday and Sunday would add to the sensation that this was one of the most out-of-kilter Mays in the history of the Indianapolis Speedway. There was the usual happiness for the successful ones, the usual disappointment and regret for those left out, but the principal overtone was irony.

The ever-fluctuating minimum estimate to make the race was now 139.3 mph. Repeatedly, drivers were called off qualifying attempts by crew members if they were slower than that. As trials roared along without letup, five successful attempts of 140 or better kept alive the impression.

On Sunday, through a rain delay of nearly 2 hours, the estimation of the ceiling persisted. Troy Ruttman had been signaled to a stop in the Novi at a 138.3 pace. Gene Hartley was called off at 138.2 and Spider Webb at 138. Webb had even gone into a brake-induced slide that ended only fifty yards from the finish line when his crew waited almost too long to halt him before he crossed the line a fourth time under his own power and thus legally completing the trial. The slide sent three crewmen scurrying over an inside retaining rail to escape.

But sometime after the twenty-third car made the field with a 138.750 mark and with only 2 hours, 45 minutes of trial time remaining, the crews of slower machines recalculated. They realized the 139.3 pilots were now scarce, with most of them already in the field, and that some of the others were down to a last qualifying chance and would be cautious. They could lower the goal.

Also, more rain appeared imminent, which inspired the crews of slower cars to gamble. Now 136s and less were accepted as the field steadily filled. The thirty-third car made the grade with only fifty-two minutes to go. Everyone who had a machine that would run at all was in line now, including those regretful guessers who had quit on faster speeds than those now being accepted. The men in line complained that cars too slow to make the field were squandering precious time on the track.

The high drama of bumping was bringing the abnormal weekend to a close. Only a fraction of an unusually small Sunday crowd of 25,000 stayed to the last minute, but they witnessed a strange twist.

Elisian was pushed away just seconds before the 6 p.m. closing gun sounded. He had only to better a 133.245 to make the grade. He took his two allowable warm-ups to gather himself and make certain the car was functioning its best. As he went by the second time the AAA official — to the astonishment of press and other spectators keeping count — flashed a yellow light to recall him.

Bewildered, Elisian came in. His owner, Pete Wales, protested heatedly to Chief Steward McQuinn, who listened and replied: "Pete, if we're wrong, we'll qualify you at midnight."

Amid the numbing last-second pressure, the AAA officials thought Elisian had crossed the finish line three times without raising his hand to signify he wanted the green flag. They had struggled with the electric timing tape from the first qualifier on that day, however. Amid strong dissent from the press, which unanimously claimed Elisian had completed just two laps, and catcalls and boos from fans across the track, the officials searched for the truth — and at 36 minutes after 6 o'clock they decided they had been wrong.

They gave Elisian his "proper chance" and Ed qualified easily, in 135.333. While cameramen and reporters gathered round him, exhilarated by a vignette out of pure fiction, Elisian was poker-faced. He finally smiled when Wales kissed him, and, dusk having arrived, a lantern somehow was produced for a gag shot. The decision had required soul-searching by AAA officials, who had a reputation for arbitrariness — but then, wasn't this an odd Speedway year anyway?

The drivers in the field seemed to be divided like passengers on a train trip — in two sections. After Chuck Weyant's 138.063 car on the inside of the ninth row, there was a drop-off to Johnny Boyd's 136.981. There was more than an eight-mile-an-hour spread from McGrath's pole sitting 142.580 to Johnny Thomson's last-place 134.113. In that disparity, many foresaw trouble; the slower cars could prove to be obstacles. Also, nearly 25 percent of the drivers were rookies — eight in all, an unusually high number. The veteran drivers knew they would have to be especially vigilant in traffic.

❦

Race day was still eight days off, but the track remained closed until Thursday, when fuel, tire, and carburetion checks would be run. It would then close again until Monday for the race. Announcements over the loud-speaker system occasionally pierced the silence amid the grounds, and the soft whir of a fan or a low-volume radio were about the only noises heard beyond garage doors.

The race was now back in the hands of the mechanics. Drivers only got in the way, like the strangers who stand in doorways in search of overheard secrets. Some of the world's best eaves-dropping — and worst manners — are displayed at the Speedway.

Not a single car qualified for the race was left whole on Monday. Every garage began again from the bottom, piecing the material together like a watch. It was good that much time remained, for inspection revealed many faulty parts or imminent failures and there was an abundance of red tags (marked, euphemistically, "discontinuities") attached to the rejected materials. Crankshafts suffered the most. Everywhere there was sawing, twisting, spraying, cleaning.

Meanwhile, the gin rummy games and idle conversations in the cafeteria flourished. Vukovich had coffee with Faulkner there one day. They chatted about nothing in particular. Then, staring into the cup, Bill said, "I don't think I'll finish the race." Walt looked at him silently. Bill changed the subject.

Wednesday evening — five days to go — Dick Hopper, Esther and Bill, and my wife and I sat at a dinner table in the quiet, table-lamp atmosphere of the Wilbur Shaw '500 Club' in downtown Indianapolis. Around them, on burnt-sand walls, hung portraits of former winners of the race. It was, as always, Bill's show, as the group talked. Some of the things that were bothering him he let out or hinted at. By turns he was intense, bitter, regretful, grateful, facetious, and self-critical.

"A guy don't make enough money out of running here," he said. "Guys think I'm a madman when I talk about making more money here. I haven't made $90,000 in the last three races here. We won everything, *everything,* in '53 — everything you can get, all but five laps, and I paid taxes on $41,000. I haven't made much over $85,000 for the last two years."

Such statements were a rebuttal to his crew members' jokes about his wealth as well as his sincere belief that race drivers were grossly underpaid for the risks they take. Then his thoughts jumped to the highly regarded Indianapolis winners of the past:

"I don't know what those other guys did to be called so great that I haven't done in a lot less time. Those are just the facts."

His companions let him talk out the anxiety that was building in him. I asked, grinning, because I didn't expect an answer, "When will you catch McGrath?"

Bill replied seriously: "I don't tell anybody what I'm going to do. When you're going to do something, don't talk about it. Just do it."

"When are you going to quit racing?"

"When I decide to quit racing, I just won't show up. I'll announce nothing."

Now Hopper suggested that Bill hang up his helmet if he earned "some loot" this year. Bill looked away, thoughtfully. He replied only indirectly, and softly:

"God, it isn't worth it, the money you make out here."

This was the third reference in three days Bill had made to the money in racing, a degree of preoccupation out of character for him. He had never before examined the "500" so narrowly. His attitude also leant support, albeit oblique, to his oft-repeated crack: "This (racing) is a hobby; I work for a living."

He went on: "A guy with a camera yaks at you; you gotta get cleaned up and put on a shirt and tie and he snaps a picture and you go home and get undressed. Hell, it isn't worth it. You go to a dinner and a guy gets up and yaks, yaks and introduces you and you say a few words and twenty minutes later no one knows what the hell went on. Everything's forgotten. They wine you and dine you and then forget you."

Manny Ayulo's name came up. When it did, Bill replied casually, "Well, here today, gone tomorrow."

I looked at Bill's eyes, now staring at the table. This was the most casual, unfeeling statement I had ever heard him make; he had said a thing he thought race drivers were supposed to say but it wasn't really his belief.

Soon came another typical Vukovich interjection, apropos of nothing under discussion:

"God, I guess I'm just obsolete. There's nothing I do but race. I'd like to do something else. You know, I've always wanted to learn to dance. I don't know why I don't. There's no better way to have fun. Esther's a great dancer."

Esther reported she had just received a letter from Marlene, which read: "Tell Daddy to stick his foot in it, I need some new clothes." They grinned at the racetrack jargon — "stick your foot in it" meant "don't be afraid to start hard on the throttle."

"That Marlene is a little lady," Bill said proudly, with a broad smile.

There was more about racing. "I got me a really good deal for next year. They don't give you nothing out here you don't earn. The biggest thrill I ever got out here was that little Keck car in '52. When we started out, from the finish line to that first corner in the first lap, the way it was running I knew we were in business ... If I never drive for that Keck again, I'll say this, there's no better guy to work for. He's strictly first cabin. He doesn't sit around and ask how do you like this and how do you like that. He just gets the best stuff or tells Crabby and them guys to get the best and that's all there is to it ... You know, there never was a combination around here that broke up and the guys did any good after that."

The next day offered the last opportunity for checking cars on the track, in motion. All but four of the thirty-three took it. Some crews left clues as to the speed they planned for the race. Bill, who would be in the middle of the second row, cruised easily at 136.7 and Travers and Coon appeared content when they wheeled the car back to its stall. Hoyt, who despite sitting on the pole position was not considered likely to make it first to the first turn, practiced starts. McGrath was primarily interested in scuffing in tires but went 138.5. The general feeling was that Jack would set the pace. Was that the speed at which he was going to do it? Faulkner cruised at 137 and later announced, "If they want to run 500 miles faster than that they can have it."

The 100-Mile-an-Hour Club held its annual banquet that night and reporters circulated among the drivers, gingerly asking who they thought would win. McGrath was the decisive choice. Only one member among the fifteen who consented to predict picked Vukovich. Then they were asked to pick one-two-three. The broader poll of the thirteen cast ballots provided a curious revelation. Bill received not one single first-place vote, but he was given second place on eleven of them. The inference was plain; drivers consider an unprecedented three consecutive victories an unlikely miracle and an improbable extension of luck — but if any man could crowd the impossible it would be Vukovich.

The dozen newspaper and radio men who had been at the Speedway the entire month took a poll among themselves. Though they displayed some contempt for the odds by voting Bill a few first-place finishes, they, too, favored McGrath.

Amid all this, Bill said to Esther: "I'm going to blow McGrath off. You just watch me."

It was a rare instance of Bill seriously boasting to Esther about what he was going to do. She let it stand without comment. Bill did, too.

However, the great majority of fans unburdened by precedent and mathematical probabilities, and who thought only of the spectacle of Vukovich annually hurtling to the front, had reached one conclusion. "Vukovich can win this every year."

⊁-⊰

It rained on Saturday and was abnormally cool. The Speedway population banded into little knots. The drivers were never far from their cars, as if they were keeping a vigil on their lifelines. Downtown, the newspapers were greeting and photographing the celebrity spectators: Dinah Shore, the entertainment star who was to kiss the winner; Latin-American diplomats; band leaders; singers; violinists; government heads; actors; athletes; auto industry tycoons.

And old race drivers, too — old race drivers, whom the gods of chance had permitted to become just that — old. Eighteen of the previous thirty-two winners of the "500" were still alive. Nine of the fourteen who were deceased had died in race accidents.

Sunday was cool, too, but the sun was sufficient to make the drivers squint as they sat in their meeting, the target of all eyes in the crowd on the Pagoda lawn. Continual prayerful references were made as Speedway and AAA officials and Shore addressed them.

The track owner told them: "I want to wish everyone in the race the best of luck … and let's all be at the banquet Tuesday night." He meant all to be there unhurt.

The medical staff chief scolded them: "You have used only about a third as much fire repellent fluid for your uniforms this year as last. Please use that fluid."

The starter reviewed the meaning of the seven flags normally employed during the race, then spent some time with an eighth — white with a red X. "This is the ambulance flag, a warning in case of an ambulance call."

The chief steward warned: "If somebody jumps the pole car, I'll have to send a pink card up to the scorer penalizing you one lap. There

The starting field lines up in proper order for the drivers' meeting the day before the race. Fluke polesitter Jerry Hoyt is front row right, accompanied by Tony Bettenhausen (center) and Jack McGrath. Vukovich is second row, center. (IMS Photos)

will be cameras there to catch the start and we can develop the picture in three to five minutes."

Shore: "This earth-bound creature will be awaiting you comets with open arms … good luck … bless you."

Their wives looked at them with expressions both proud and fearful.

The drivers gave all their attention to information pertinent to their welfare but otherwise sat listlessly throughout the outpouring of words.

It wasn't really boredom; more like submission. They were captives at a tense time when they wanted the hours to be their own. Bill, at times, appeared the most removed of all. The meeting over, nothing more was left to be done but wait.

Bill had one more psychological dart to throw. He aimed it at the man the experts — though not the people — picked to beat him, Jack McGrath.

"McGraver," he said, as he liked to call McGrath, "I'm going to give you a big slide tomorrow — because you don't like it." Jack answered amiably: "Okay."

Bill spent little time in the garage that day, but he asked Travers to mount and install a thermos jug in the cockpit. Travers spent some precious time installing it.

As the afternoon ticked on, several of the drivers and their wives joined officials and press and radio at Firestone's customary lawn picnic outside the southeast turn, a pleasant, casual, low-key affair that provided a welcome pause before the tornado of activity that would come the next day. Esther persuaded Bill to attend. Having agreed, he hurried over, then chided Alice Hanks about the circuitous route her husband, Sam, took to reach the picnic: "No wonder your old man doesn't know how to get around this racetrack."

"Bill!" Esther exclaimed, rebuking him sharply.

Bill grinned widely, which lightened the mood around him, but a few moments later, alone with Esther, he dropped his party pose.

"I'll be glad when this rat race is over."

Esther's voice was soft and gentle, instantly responding to his mood. "You feel like going home, don't you?" She meant Fresno.

"Yeah," he said, almost wistfully.

"It will only take me a minute to pack," Esther said. She knew he was troubled; she was anxious as well. Her tone was comforting, but she did not press the point. It had to be his decision.

Bill turned and walked away without another word.

"This place will always give you a thrill, I'll clue you."

Chasing History

It was time for Bill to change into driving dress. The garage was the emptiest it had been all month. The car and its accoutrements had been taken to the pit early in the morning. He wouldn't see his crew for a while yet, unless one of them had to return for something forgotten. The crew had much to do before they turned their attention to him.

Jim Travers and Frank Coon had to heat the oil and fire the engine and listen to sounds and check parts. Mel Straw and Jim Nairn set out tire-changing hammers and wheel jacks. Stu Hilborn examined his chart for scoring and fuel computations. The crew also had taken on a late addition, Herb Porter. He had been the chief mechanic for the car driven by Paul Russo, but the mechanical failure that caused Russo to crash on a practice lap earlier in the month made him available. Now with Vukovich's crew he examined and re-examined the fueling tank and checked the pressure gauge and made sure the tank was positioned at the precise place behind the wall for the hose to reach the car.

During the pit stops Porter would refuel, Coon would cover the exhaust pipe and change the right rear, Travers would be responsible for the left rear, Nairn the left front, and Straw the right front. The complete service would have to be done in around fifty seconds for a pit stop that would help win the race, and each frequently eyed his section of the car as if it were the only part that existed.

Bill put on a white T-shirt, white duck pants, and bowling shoes. He tied the tail of the shirt to his undershorts with bits of string to keep

Dinah Shore and the Chevrolet pace car were featured attractions at the 1955 "500." (Bob Gates collection)

the shirt from working its way out and billowing in the strong slipstream of the race. He decided to wear only a thin cotton shirt despite the cold day, even though other drivers wore jackets or long-sleeved worsted wool uniforms.

He took off his ring and placed it with his silver-dollar money clip in a corner of the work bench. He had carried a silver dollar given to him by Fred Gerhardt for good luck for two races, then had it made into a clip. Luck would have to be sacrificed to remove sharp metal edges in the cockpit.

He examined his crash helmet, turned it over, put his goggles and gloves in it, and set it aside. There was still considerable time.

It was quiet in the garage area, which now was strictly policed at the gates. The sounds of shuffling feet outside Bill's garage were muted. Occasionally an opponent stopped briefly in the doorway to wish him luck and Bill returned the wishes. Only a few confidants tarried with him. I was one, along with Harley Copp, an urbane Ford Motor Company research engineer whom Bill had met in Mexico and developed a mutual admiration. We stopped in a little after 9. We let Bill do most of the talking, but only when he felt like it. We stood by silently, prodding him infrequently. He talked easily, of little things. He was relaxed and he grinned easily when one or the other needled him. He toyed around with the stiff elastic exerciser he had stretched all month, continually preparing himself.

"We got a letter from our little girl," Bill announced, still thinking of home. "She's getting real clothes conscious. She's a little lady. She asked Esther to 'tell Daddy to stick his foot in it, 'cause I need some new clothes.'"

The thought of Marlene's emergence into the teenage years and her use of track slang pleased him greatly and he chuckled, his face lighting.

The approach of the race weighed heavily on the minds of the two visitors, and they brought the conversation back to it.

"Remember, Billy," Copp said, "take it easy for the first three to five laps. There's no point in running the first five laps midget-style with 195 more to go."

"I won't push it too hard, but I'll be leading the race before ten laps," Bill said. "This is my racetrack. You have to show 'em who is boss either at the beginning or the end. It's a hell of a lot easier to show 'em at the beginning." His expression was serious, almost severe.

Then his mood lightened again. "I don't think I'll race today. I've got enough money.

"Hell," he went on, "I waited until I was too old to come to Indianapolis. I'm 36. I could have won this go lotsa times and be telling my kids all about it. Hell, back in '48 it scared hell out of me to think about it."

Then he grew serious again. Now he stood stiffly erect, feet apart, the exerciser hanging across his shoulders. He looked squarely at the two:

"This place will always give you a thrill, I'll clue you."

———

I wanted to stay longer in the garage but had to leave time for the slow struggle through the crowd and the climb to the press box on the Paddock roof. I offered my hand. Bill took it.

"Luck, Bill. Hurry back."

"Thanks."

But the handshake. This was different. Bill normally had a rather odd, limp-wristed, weak grip, letting the other do the holding, a hand shake incongruous in one who clutched a race car so tightly. But now he wrapped his fingers around, held on firmly an instant. His voice was almost inaudible, and his eyes looked sad. I walked away trying to translate.

Soon Bill's other companion left, and he walked out to the track to join his crew. He greeted them and looked over the car, then dropped his helmet into the cockpit. Outsiders, half of them carrying cameras, began interrupting to wish him well or to ask an unknowing question.

The pits were thick with humanity. The Purdue marching band, with color guard, majorettes and enormous drum riding a pickup truck, were parading. The short-skirted girls stepped briskly. There would be no fainting from the heat this chilly morning.

The stands were slow to fill, undoubtedly because many wished to wait in warm cars. But Esther had arrived, sitting across the track from the pits alongside Dorcas Thompson, composed.

Bill sat in his car to pass more time. Esther, eyes riveted on her man, noticed that his gaze followed the majorettes as they pranced by. "I'm going to give him the devil about that when he gets home," she said, with a chuckle. "I guess he's checking to see if that is really leg makeup or a tan," Dorcas said with a grin.

Bill got out of the car. He was restless. He walked to Bettenhausen, took Tony's hand, held it with both of his.

"Tony, I wish you luck, and I really mean it."

He walked away and Bettenhausen also pondered the change in Bill's grip and tone of voice.

The band launched into "On the Banks of the Wabash." Now the signal was given to push the cars onto the track and back to the starting line.

Travers needled, reminding him of the thermos jug that had been installed. "We're going to push your soda fountain back now, Bill."

With cars moving toward the track amid the backdrop of music, everyone began to move a little faster, pulses quickening. Forty-five minutes to go. The sky was dark gray and threatening. The optimistic forecast of dry weather appeared errant. The wind continually shifted, blowing at 20 to 25 mph.

As the drivers scurried to the track, Vukovich and Elisian crossed paths. Ed sensed Bill's serious mood but wanted to inject something light.

"We gonna have steaks and whiskey afterwards?" he asked.

"You just take your time out there, Ed," Vukovich said. "We're going to have steak and whiskey. Watch the wind. It's pretty rough. I'm always afraid someone's going to get hurt. Some guys try too damn hard and get into trouble."

They parted and headed for their machines.

A public address announcer, Irish Horan, began his interviews of drivers and mechanics at the starting line. He stopped Bill and announced: "We have a stroke of luck today, folks — Billy Vukovich." This was the first time Bill had been brought to the microphone before the race. Heretofore he had kept a wary eye open and evaded the announcer.

"This is going to be a rough race," he said, and left it at that.

The band and color guard began a "Parade of Nations" in front of the front stretch grandstands, carrying huge flags of twenty-two North and South American countries. Police motorcycle officers followed, leading twenty-two replicas of the convertible pace car. In them rode the ambassadors, officially escorted by the Secretary of the Army, Robert Stevens, with Speedway host Tony Hulman.

Ka-booomb! The first of the salute bombs went off. Twenty-five minutes more.

The stewards drove off in the pace car, taking Dinah Shore, wearing red coat and white dress, with them, for the final inspection of the track. The drivers were summoned forward, to assemble hurriedly for a group picture in front of the Pagoda. Some agreed because they wanted a reminder of these tense minutes before the race. Others ignored the call because they found the minutes too nerve-wracking to hold still.

Vukovich talked to his crew. Porter said to him lightly, "Hurry back, Bill. We've got some cold beer in the icebox."

"Will an hour-and-a-half suit you?" Bill asked.

The band struck up the national anthem, which stilled the murmur in the stands, the crackle of the public address system, the patter of the crews, and the pounding of hurrying feet.

A photographer asked Hopkins to pose with Vukovich, who, getting set for the picture, yawned behind his gloved hand. Mel Straw thought, *This is a nervous man?*

Another bomb. Fifteen minutes now.

Bill tugged at his gloves in an exaggerated motion for his crew, aping the ostentatious glove-donning performed by some drivers. "I gotta get nervous," he cracked.

He then turned serious as he faced the crew: "What lap do you want me to catch him?" He meant McGrath.

The crew was aghast. Several spoke at once, trying to tone him down.

"Hey, Bill, that's impossible. Don't try it. He's popped."

They knew McGrath had the fastest car and he was in an advantageous position outside in the front row. With nitro in his car, Jack would be even more difficult to overtake immediately.

Vukovich snarled back: "Listen! The sonuvabitch doesn't like to be run close to and I'm going to run close to him."

The melancholy notes of "Taps" rose in the air. The poignant melody of the trumpets seemed to suggest not so much a moment of silence for those who had lost their lives in war as a prayer for the living who were about to tempt fate.

The band marched off the track. Now, as it played "Back Home Again in Indiana," Dinah Shore sang with great feeling. She asked the fans to join her in the second chorus. The response was tingling. Everyone stood. Esther didn't sing. Instead, a prayer ran through her mind.

Another bomb. The traditional balloons, 10,000 of them, were released from a tent in the infield, rising to provide a soothing canopy of color against the gray sky, only to rapidly drift away in the wind.

Bombs followed in staccato now and drivers, tensing, stepped into their cars, this time to stay.

◆—◆

In front of Bill, to the left, was Jerry Hoyt. Jerry wanted to race so badly that one year he took his Army furlough during May so he could try to qualify for the "500." Directly ahead of Bill, Tony Bettenhausen, father of four who in seventeen years of racing had twenty-one accidents, his body tormented from skull to ankles. To the right in that first row was McGrath, for whom Bill had a special affection and respect, but still had promised privately to "blow off" and "run close to." Immediately to the left of Bill, Agabashian, perhaps the most articulate of the breed, yet still unable to explain freely why he raced. This was his ninth "500." To the right of Bill, Hanks, who had competed in more "500s" than anyone, ready for his tenth. Sam lived comfortably from owning an apartment house and selling autos. But he wanted to race.

In the row behind Bill, Faulkner. Walt had once tried to describe why he raced.

"There's ego involved. Maybe we've got more of it than other people and feed on it. I used to get a big charge out of getting my name in the paper. Strangers would stop me on the street, and I'd tell myself, *Well, Walt, if you die tomorrow, you've left a little mark.* I ate the publicity stuff up — until I got hurt my first time.

"Then I lay in the hospital a long time and I began to think. We're all that way, and we come to realize that there's more to it than that. People ask me if I'm scared. You're damned right; I've been scared a lot of times. And don't let any race driver tell you he's never been scared. But you go right on because you like it. I've been near death three times, but I still want to go at it. You can drive around the track and go pretty good and then you get faster and faster and you begin to say to yourself, *I'm master of this machine* — ego again — and that ol' feeling starts moving up from your belly.

"Maybe it's competition, too. Maybe you run pretty good and faster than the next guy and outsmart him — and you kinda grin to yourself. I like life and I want to live as long as anyone, but …"

Behind Bill, Cal Niday, more proof that there is no telling what size or shape a race car driver will be. Cal had a wooden leg, had been a barber and beauty shop operator, stood just 5 feet, 4 inches, and wore a wispy mustache.

"I got into racing because I wanted to prove to myself that I was as good as anyone else — the people that I ran around with — that I wasn't handicapped because of my leg. I wasn't trying to prove anything to other people. I was just trying to prove something to myself."

In the fourth row, Bryan, who usually gave a glib answer — "for money" — when asked why he raced, but once said he probably would race for nothing, which he did when he started. In the fifth row, Bob Sweikert, who said, "I'm the twitchy type. Racing gives me an outlet. I'm nervous. I'm not a religious man, but I think that God wanted me to do what I'm doing. Or why should I be doing it? And if it's His desire that I be crippled up in it that's the way it's going to be."

Farther back, in the eighth row, Al Keller, one of the eight driving his first "500" in a dirt-track type car that had a hand brake on the outside, which meant that in an emergency he would have to take one hand off the wheel to get to the brake.

Next to him, Ray Crawford, another rookie, another enigma. He was already rich from a supermarket fortune. Why was he racing?

"Racing is like being on dope," he said. "You know what you're doing is crazy, but you don't know how to get the desire out of your blood. The car is an extension of yourself — you feel part of it. The engine is hot and running sweet. You're not conscious of the noise, but you know it's roaring. The track slips away in a blur. You're running close to the bone. Then suddenly you find tears on your face. You're crying with elation. That's racing."

Also in the eighth row, the steady and durable Art Cross: "You don't do any worrying. Guys come around and start needling. They tell you how they're going to blow you off. They don't fool you. They're trying to build up their own confidence ... It's mental aggravation that induces physical fatigue at first. Sure, it's hot and wearisome but you try to keep telling yourself you can stand it. You've got to keep your mind from defeating you. But when your problems get too great your mind will tell you you've had it … You don't worry about who is involved in an accident when the yellow light goes on, if he went over the wall, if he's hurt. Not then. You look to see what's caused the yellow to be turned on, if you can, and what it means to you, trouble to avoid. You don't worry about your safety out there, about the wife and kiddies; not then."

In the ninth row, another first timer in the "500," Fresno's Johnny Boyd, who had spun out unhurt on his first qualifying attempt. He faced it calmly: "I have been a race driver for nine years. Don't think I'm cocky, but I have to believe that I'm a good driver, as good as any of them, or I wouldn't be worth my salt. I guess I am worried about where I'll finish — and how much money I'll make."

Behind him, in the middle of the tenth row, Elisian. A young man at loose ends, who didn't articulate it well, but by his actions considered racing to be a compulsion. And starboard of him, Rodger Ward, who used a bigger word than most, but it meant the same: "Exhilaration."

≫—≪

Finally, the call to action from Speedway owner Tony Hulman: "Gentlemen, start your engines!"

Crew members jumped as though frightened, inserted cranks, flicked on battery switches with shaking thumbs, tensely clutched vibrating starter shafts, winded by excitement. As the engines coughed, and then caught, they hastily withdrew the cranks, held up their arms to signify they were ready. All hands raised, the cars began their slow roll-away, behind the pace car, moving into proper formation. The crews raced for their pit wall positions, to be there when the cars came back around.

The sight of the rolling men lifted the emotion in the grandstands and bleachers to another level. Everyone stood, straining forward, involuntarily releasing a vast shudder of anticipation. In the grandstand on the first curve, where it always appears to the occupants that the cars are hurtling straight into their laps until the last-second veer-off, there was the annual cry, directed at those up front: "Sit down! Sit down!"

When the thirty-three cars returned to the start/finish line for their flying start, they catapulted from it like creatures with minds of their own. McGrath was first into the first turn, Bettenhausen second, Hoyt third — and then Vukovich.

At the end of the first lap McGrath's cream-colored rocket was still in front, then Bettenhausen and Hoyt, with Vukovich's blue bolt growling at Hoyt's tail. The engines of the first three abruptly lowered their pitch as they approached the curve, but Bill's throttle still revealed who wanted it the most. He still wasn't lifting. He flashed by Hoyt and Bettenhausen in the back stretch. At three laps, McGrath was still in front, Vukovich second, Bettenhausen third.

They went through the two south banks, Vukovich closing steadily, and in the smooth, back straightaway an extra spasm of fury carried him past McGrath. In just eight miles, in traffic, he had overtaken a car a mile-and-a-half faster than his. As they emerged from the fourth turn and into the main straightaway, the fans let out a convulsive roar when they saw the blue car emerge first, leading the yellow one. The two crossed the line to complete the fourth lap, and Bill Vukovich was ruling the field in the Indianapolis 500-Mile Race for the fourth straight year. He was ahead by thirty yards. Surprisingly, he waved a hand to the applauding crowd, another atypical Vukovich gesture.

He pulled a few feet farther ahead of McGrath, but he couldn't feel comfortable. There was too much car and too much man pursuing him for that. Oblivious to the other thirty-one in the battle, the two ground away at each other, lap after scorching, screeching lap, at better than 135 mph.

McGrath began slowly but steadily regaining lost ground. An unnatural light blue smoke trailed from his car. Their respective crews left them alone so as not to distract them. Resolving their duel was necessary before either crew could plot a course.

After fourteen laps, Bill had caught the trailers in the field. Before the fifteenth was over, McGrath had closed off the space once separating him from Bill. As they streaked down the home straightaway, at 180 mph, McGrath put his front wheels ahead. Bill, on the inside, fought him for the length of the chute. As they battled to the curve, McGrath edged ahead. He jostled his way down to the white line, the warning boundary that marks the edge of the racetrack proper, beyond which there was only asphalt roughage, loose dirt and sparse grass. A car racing in it courted disaster. McGrath hugged the line to keep Vukovich behind him.

He had "sawed off" Bill, claiming the groove, ethically his. Bill refused to accept the inevitable. As a hundred thousand fans watched, Vukovich sent his car under McGrath, all four wheels below the white line. Some stared open-mouthed, others gasped; all stood frozen, affixed by the drama.

Impatient in a race that still had 462 miles to go, Vukovich's will searched for any path toward the lead it could find, even if it meant pursuing a course fraught with peril. He had recently at various times expressed an uneasiness about his dangerous profession, yet while immersed in it dared to add to the risks.

He didn't, of course, wrest the lead from McGrath, though his plunge into the shorter path gave him a split second's creep-up on Jack. But his path had little traction and he had to return to the racing surface. McGrath, discovering Bill to his left in that forbidding spot was startled. He later recalled thinking, *He's got more guts than I have. He wants to win more than he wants to live. I want to live a little longer. There is more to life than winning.*

Bill was not to be denied in the back stretch, however, and he was in front again as they came around to the main straight. He saluted his pit, as if to tell his crew he was in command.

He was for nine more laps — through a yellow light for an Agabashian spin-out — but on the twenty-fifth McGrath once again got past him. They continued as if in tandem and completed the twenty-sixth together but as they plunged again into the separator — the first turn — Vukovich inched ahead. There, he stayed.

Though he piled second upon hard-won second to his advantage, he showed no restraint as he gobbled up the slower cars in the field. Once he came upon Crawford only a few feet from the wall and went roaring through the impossibly small opening between Ray and the cement. Crawford, frightened by Bill's daring, whispered, "Jesus God!" McGrath reflected, *He's doing things I never saw him do before.* And once, when Bill went streaking past Elisian, Ed looked over and thought, *He's driving like an angry bull.* But on another lap when Vukovich was passing Elisian he waved to Ed and gave him a flick of his hand, meaning "Come on!"

In time — in almost impossibly quick time for Indianapolis — Vukovich was into the fresh air and in control. As he lengthened his escape from the pack, he left his closest challengers in their own tightly bunched skirmish for second — McGrath, Sweikert, Hanks, Bryan, and Cross. The smoke from McGrath's car was increasing, however. By the fortieth lap Bill held a ten-second lead and sunlight was peering through the dark clouds. By the fiftieth lap — 125 miles — he had run away to a twenty-second margin. What with the faithful music his car was making, coupled with his proven endurance, another victory seemed only a matter of time.

15

"Someday, they'll have to pick me up off a racetrack."

Nowhere to Go

With Vukovich routinely clicking off laps and leading comfortably, the spectators settled back into their seats or — noon at hand — broke out lunch and diverted their attention from the track. The picnic atmosphere added a glow to the day's festivities.

Atop the Paddock, occupying the full length of the main straightaway opposite the pits, 300 press and radio representatives from every corner of the Western Hemisphere worked feverishly, typing out lap-by-lap results, jotting down numbers and positions, making pit stop observations, and absorbing the stream of memos from the Speedway's teletype machines.

Vukovich set a track record for the first 125 miles (50 laps), 136.212 mph. He lapped the seventh-place driver, Faulkner, on Lap 51. On lap 53, McGrath, running second, finally signaled to his crew he would come in to check on the cause of the smoke streaming from his tailpipe. They lifted the hood and immediately determined that he would have to drop out of the race and began pushing the car to the garage area.

When Vukovich drove by his pit, crew members pointed to McGrath standing in the pits and Bill nodded in acknowledgement. Please that the nearest threat had been eliminated, they began to track the lead over Sweikert, peering up the track to watch him glide out of the fourth turn and charting each completed lap as he zoomed by them. He was driving more smoothly now, no longer needing to bully the car with his comfortable lead. It was if it had quit fighting him.

Esther talked happily with Dorcas, but she didn't miss a lap.
'Round.

And 'round.

… And 'round.

Each reappearance by Vukovich brought pleasure to the fans, for his spirit had come through even to those who had never been closer to him than a grandstand seat or a newspaper picture or article.

Other drivers, of course, possessed a flaming spirit, and other drivers were daring. What separated him from the pack was an overused word that genuinely applied to him: Integrity. In a day and time of duplicity and hypocrisy and conning, Bill Vukovich came closest to being the completely honest man. If he didn't like a thing or a man, he shunned it or him. He punctured balloons. He told the truth and didn't fear the consequences. He cared not if he incurred a man's displeasure, for he desired only to maintain his self-respect.

Integrity, enhanced by limitless courage and hard-earned physical endowment, separated Bill Vukovich from the pack of humanity. Other men saw in him the full man they could be if they dared. They reacted either with mean, small envy or drew moral courage from him.

There was a wishful spectator identification with Vukovich, beyond the average Walter Mitty longing. Here was a man who dared to hew his own path and a generation of conformists, compromisers, and conventionalists responded, some unconsciously.

Bill finished Lap 56. He now had led seventy-one percent of the laps he had run in the "500," by far the best among all drivers who had competed in at least five races. Of his 675 laps on the track, he had led 485. Of his 1,688 miles on it, he had led in 1,212. No one was within sight of that kind of dominance. The argument could reasonably be made that he was the greatest driver ever to compete in the 500-Mile Race. If not for his horrible fate in 1952 when his steering failed with less than nine laps to go, he would be winner of three consecutive races — and headed for a fourth.

He began Lap 57 by sailing by Elisian again and entered the south turns unhampered by traffic. Boyd, in front of him, was his next quarry.

Just ahead of Boyd was Keller. As he emerged from the second turn, he eyed the backstretch ahead of him.

Trouble!

Rodger Ward was stopped in the middle of the track, having broken an axle, spun, and slammed into the outside retaining rail halfway up the backstretch. Keller, following Ward, reached for his hand brake. The sudden application sent him into a loop to the left just barely into the infield, but he seemed to have enough control to stay there.

There was sufficient space between Keller and Ward for Boyd and Vukovich to race through. Bill angled to the right to use the opening. He didn't lift his foot from the throttle. In a split second he would be home free.

Suddenly, Keller's car shot back across the track, spinning, and crashed into Boyd. The impact sent Boyd to the right and into Bill's path. Vukovich, full throttle, left with no options, ran into the rear of Boyd's car. Both cars catapulted into the air. The bottom of Boyd's car hit the pedestrian bridge running over the track and flipped down the track. A split-second later Vukovich's car went airborne. It catapulted insanely twenty feet into the air and cartwheeled eleven times — and severed the thread that holds the Damoclean sword hanging over the head of a race driver.

Vukovich's car comes to rest outside the backstretch wall. This photo ran in newspapers throughout the country, many of them pointing out his hand sticking out of the cockpit. (Joe Young collection)

The "death car," back in the garage area. It would be restored and compete in the following year's race. (IMS Photos)

One Year Later

A few nights after the running of the 1956 race, two other Indianapolis sportswriters and I were enjoying a pleasant cruise by a lake. A fourth man, the driver, was a race fan. All were awaiting an automobile race the next day and wondering what the event would bring to some men's lives. The fan suddenly turned to us and asked:

"What was there about Vukovich's death that brought such great reaction? Other race drivers have been killed."

I had not cared to talk about the crash for the past year. But at that moment I looked up and said, quietly, "I'll tell you."

"He was quite a guy, and there isn't a day in my life that I don't think about him. And there isn't a day in my life that I don't think what might have been. We should have won that race four times in a row. But 'if' in racing is a big word." — Jim Travers

Epilogue

By Mark Montieth

"If" was the biggest word of all in Bill Vukovich's abbreviated life.

If not for terribly bad luck in 1952 and tragically bad luck in 1955, he would have won the Indianapolis 500 four consecutive times. Forget about good luck, he didn't need that. His talent would have been enough.

Imagine how he would be regarded still today if not for those gargantuan "ifs" his legendary mechanic, Jim Travers, referenced. Only four drivers have won the "500" four times, but nobody has won more than two consecutively. If not for the failure of a 50-cent steering wheel cotter pin in 1952 that had not been strengthened by heat treatment as it should have been, and the fatal backstretch accident not of his making in 1955, Vukovich likely would own that accomplishment and reign as the race's premier legend.

And who's to say he wouldn't have won more of them had he survived in '55? Maybe he would have retired as some predicted and settled into a quiet life in Fresno running his two gas stations/repair shops. But thinking about retiring and actually retiring are two vastly different things, as athletes and others in the entertainment industry prove so often. For many, the lure of an adrenaline rush is too much to resist for long. The money isn't bad, either.

All we know for sure is that the fluky backstretch accident on Lap 57 of the 1955 Indianapolis 500 ended one life and dramatically altered several others. The ripple effects are still felt today.

❦

The radio broadcast of the 1955 race, originated by WIBC in Indianapolis and carried by 237 affiliates in 48 states and over the Armed Forces Radio Network to a worldwide audience of an estimated 40 million listeners, told the story of Vukovich's fate in real time.

Sid Collins was the host announcer, expert in his ability to deliver the broadcast with upright formality in a rich baritone voice while smoothly incorporating reports from six other announcers positioned around the track, in the pits and in the Pagoda to give updated standings as the race progressed.

After the traditional pre-race pageantry of bombs, balloons and bands, the race was dramatic from the drop of the green flag. When Vukovich quickly moved from fifth to first, Jim Shelton exclaimed, "I'll tell you one thing, Sid, this Vukovich is an amazing man!" When his primary competitor, Jack McGrath, soon had blue smoke spewing from the back of his car, Vukovich's odds for winning a third consecutive race improved dramatically.

Vukovich's lead was 10.5 seconds after 48 laps, at which time Collins interviewed Dinah Shore — "brown-eyed and honey-haired"— who had sung "Back Home Again in Indiana" before the race and would plant the traditional kiss on the winner afterward. Amid their casual conversation he asked about her outfit, which she described as a white cotton dress with gypsy red trim, white gloves and a bright red coat — the same colors as the Chevrolet pace car that day, they made sure to point out. Revving up her southern charm, she expressed amazement at what she was witnessing in her first view of the event, exclaiming, "This is the most unbelievably exhilarating occasion!"

Down in the Vukovich pit meanwhile, the crew was feeling its own sense of exhilaration. They had just refueled, and their driver had a commanding lead. He had run the fastest lap in race history, 141.35, while overtaking McGrath and had taken a lead that reached 17 seconds at one point. With McGrath out of the race because of magneto failure, it appeared nobody could catch him.

"Everything was on the up and up again, it was just going beautiful," Travers recalled years later.

Once the casual conversation with Dinah Shore had finished, Collins called in Charlie Brockman for an update of the leaders. Brockman reported Vukovich still led after 56 laps, but then stopped after noticing the yellow caution light was lit. He took it upon himself to turn the broadcast over to Jack Shapiro on the backstretch, bypassing Collins, the broadcast's usual signal-caller.

Shapiro offered the first report of a five-car accident, describing how it transpired from his viewpoint, adding, "There is much trouble back here." He mentioned the wrecked cars of Rodger Ward, Ed Elisian, Johnny Boyd and Al Keller but couldn't identify the fifth.

"There's a car burning, and I cannot tell the number from here … it's off the track about 100 yards from me and I cannot see what car it is … they are putting out the fire now," Shapiro said. Moments later, he summarized the scene: "It's mayhem!"

As Shapiro continued talking, hoping to learn the identity of the fifth car in the accident, Collins interrupted and suggested he drop his microphone and go find out. Collins then cut to a commercial for Chevrolet. By the time the broadcast resumed, Collins had deduced that Vukovich was the other driver in the accident because he had not seen him in the parade of cars circling amid the yellow light. Brockman confirmed it, having seen Vukovich's crew members desperately looking for their driver.

"They look very disheartened at this moment," Brockman said. "We have been watching for Vukovich, so very apparently Vukovich is in some sort of trouble, and we don't know where."

After Collins gave a rundown of major crashes in previous "500s" Shapiro came back with an update:

"I know what happened all right. The car that's burning is Car No. 4, we're pretty sure. I can't get across the track, but everyone seems to tell me it's Bill Vukovich's car that's still burning. Now, Bill, I understand, is in the ambulance, he's probably on the way now to be checked. I do not know what happened to him."

Shapiro offered to give another description of the accident, but Collins brought in pit reporter Luke Walton, who interviewed McGrath, who by now was out of the race because of mechanical trouble. Collins then returned the broadcast to Shapiro:

"What happened out here, precisely now, Car 27 with Rodger Ward got into trouble, started to slide, went sideways. Car 39 by Boyd went up and over him, bounced 50 feet. Then 68 went into the infield, Elisian, then 42 same thing, Keller, then Vukovich evidently going to the outside went over the outside wall and that car is still burning over there."

Shapiro pronounced Ward, Elisian, Keller and Boyd to be "all right," but added, "What happened to Bill Vukovich, we have no information."

Shapiro went on to describe the accident as "a horrible thing to watch," while Collins said Vukovich was "perhaps trying a little bit too hard" — a judgement based on Vukovich's reputation as an aggressive driver rather than anything Collins could have witnessed.

After Brockman listed the official leaders after 50 laps, Shapiro described Vukovich's part in the accident in greater detail from descriptions given to him by race officials. Vukovich's car, he said, had bounced over the outside wall on the backstretch, landed on a car, bounced end over end for another 50 to 60 feet, and landed upside-down. The safety crew was just now putting out the fire and Vukovich had been placed in an ambulance.

After another commercial for Chevrolet, Collins gave the Speedway's official description of the accident, adding, "we certainly hope everybody is OK." He then asked Brockman for another leader report. Brockman obliged but called it "strictly a guess." The broadcast continued routinely under the yellow light condition with cars still circling the track at highway speeds. Greg Smith offered a report from the south end of the pits, adding that the drivers there were "very anxiously" awaiting information on Vukovich. An interview with Freddie Agabashian in the north pit followed, then Collins talked with three-time winner Mauri Rose from his broadcast booth. Still no report on Vukovich, Collins added.

Another Chevrolet commercial was followed by more time-filling coverage. Shelton said the early laps were setting up "the greatest race ever, before the accident." Back and forth, Collins and his broadcast crew kept the air waves humming. They talked about the attendance, the celebrities on hand, and the lap leaders. There were interviews from the pits with drivers out of the race, and then Collins brought in a guest to his broadcast booth: violinist Florian ZaBach, who had completed a 12-show engagement at a local nightclub and stayed over to watch his first race.

The soft-spoken ZaBach, apparently unaware of the severity of the backstretch accident, mentioned that Vukovich — which he pronounced Yoo-ko-vich — had long been his favorite driver. The *Star* had published a photo four days before the race of ZaBach sitting in the pace car while Vukovich, wearing a flannel shirt and white painter's cap, stood by and pointed out something in the cockpit.

"In the last week I got to know him personally and enjoy what he's doing out here very, very much," ZaBach said.

Collins thanked ZaBach for his time. "You're a real sweetheart to have me," ZaBach said.

And then without hesitation Collins delivered the dreaded update:

"Fans, we have some very, very disheartening news to relate to you. An official report from the Speedway hospital … in broadcasting this race in our eighth consecutive year, we have never had to make such an announcement and we are most regretful. Bill Vukovich, three-time winner of the 500-mile race, almost, trying for his third consecutive today, trapped in his car in the backstretch, was injured fatally. Bill Vukovich has died as a result of injuries suffered on the backstretch in the accident reported to you earlier on this broadcast.

"With deep regret to all of you listeners throughout the nation, and especially to those in Fresno, California, his hometown, and most particularly to us who know him, who knew him … we have lost a very good friend.

"The race is the thing, it is their sport, it is their chosen profession and their life's blood. And as they pass away the sport continues, as it does in front of us. And Charlie, perhaps you can bring us up to date on the standings at the present time."

Indeed, the race continued. Brockman provided the update, adding, "and of course everyone is disheartened here today with the loss of a great friend as Sid has said in Bill Vukovich." Brockman pointed out Vukovich was just the second former winner to lose his life during the race and had perished in nearly the same place on the track as the first, Floyd Roberts, in 1939.

He then ran through the list of drivers killed since Shorty Cantlon in the 1947 race and from there the broadcast continued routinely.

※-※

Esther Vukovich, per her race-day routine, took two pills that morning to calm her nerves before heading to the track with her host, Dorcas Thompson. Just a few days earlier, Esther had told a local society page columnist that "you never get away from the anxiety; it hurts a little more as time goes on."

Dorcas did not enjoy attending the race, either, but went as a favor to Esther. Bill, too. Esther wanted a companion and Bill urged her to go "in case something happens." And now it had. When the yellow light came on — one that would last 27 minutes, 10 seconds — Esther immediately noticed her husband was not among the parade of drivers slowly circling the track.

"It's him," she said to Dorcas. "Something's happened. Let's go."

They left their seats, found a police officer, and were escorted to the first-aid station near the garage area to seek information. Told only that Bill had been involved in a serious accident, she was given a sedative. Lee Wallard, the 1951 winner, drove them to the infield track hospital but they were kept waiting in the car for five minutes. The track's hospital personnel were frantically busy because of the accident that had involved four other drivers. And, perhaps, nobody wanted to be the one to tell her.

By that time, Vukovich's fate was well-known within the Speedway's inner circle. He quite obviously was dead when pulled from the car, so the ambulance driver was instructed to take him directly to the Conkle

Funeral Home in Speedway — a right-hand turn out of the track — rather than the track hospital or Methodist Hospital downtown, a left turn. Esther did not know that, however. As Carolyn Pickering reported in the *Star*, Esther was overwhelmed by the combination of her anxiety and the sedative when she was finally allowed inside the track hospital. She slumped into a cot while Dorcas sat nearby. Finally, Henry Banks, a recently retired "500" veteran, who was accompanied by a local pastor, delivered the news.

Esther lay on the cot for about 30 more minutes while hospital personnel tended to the other accident victims. According to newspaper accounts, Boyd sat smoking a cigarette, in obvious pain. Ward grimaced as his arm injury was treated. Elisian wandered around in a daze. Keller was unscathed physically but in shock, hugging his wife. A spectator, Richard Wolfe of Indianapolis, had a fractured clavicle from having been hit with one of Vukovich's tires while seated in a Jeep outside the wall.

Later, after the race had resumed, Niday was brought in, his clothes torn to shreds, his face a "bloody, charred mess." His wife, Elsie, collapsed outside.

Esther finally went outside with Dorcas to sit inside a canvas tent within a fenced-off area outside the hospital. Both were in a state of shock. Vukovich's older brother, Mike, soon joined them, running into the tent and collapsing into Dorcas' arms with tears streaming down his face.

Out in Fresno, Billy Jr. and Marlene Vukovich were staying at the family home with relatives. Years later, in an ESPN Sports Century documentary on their father, Billy Jr. recalled receiving the news:

"They come by, part of the family, and they said, 'Billy, we want you to come with us.' I said, 'My dad's all right, don't worry about it.' I was 11 years old. I pictured the car in the infield with him standing behind it with an engine fire. And when they announced on TV that my dad was gone, boy that just hit me like ... in fact, I actually think I blacked out for like 10 seconds."

"You always think your dad's invincible," Marlene added. "You always think it can never happen to me."

Vukovich's other brother, Eli, was listening on the radio at his home in Fresno. The severity of the accident became obvious to him as the trackside reports progressed and he let out his anxiety by running into his backyard, pounding a fist into his hand, and screaming. "He knew something was wrong," Eli's wife told *The Fresno Bee*. "He couldn't control himself, naturally. The shock was almost too much for him. We were all stunned."

Another *Bee* article said Eli turned off the radio and went to bed after learning his brother had died. Billy Jr. and Marlene reportedly were put in bed as well.

The news coverage of fatalities in those days would be considered sensationalistic by today's standards. The banner headlines on Page 1s throughout Indianapolis, Fresno and other cities were big, bold and blunt. Some ran in all caps, such as "VUKY DEAD IN PILEUP" and "VUKY BURNS TO DEATH IN FIVE-CAR SMASHUP." That one was followed by a subhead that read, "Flaming Death Of Vukovich Ends Colorful 17-Year Racing Career." One newspaper photo showed track personnel carrying Vukovich's body, covered by a blanket, on a stretcher toward an ambulance. Another showed his car resting upside-down, still spewing smoke. His right arm was barely visible outside of the cockpit, a detail pointed out in the caption to make sure everyone noticed. That photo has been highly circulated, although the Speedway's photo shop refuses to sell it today.

The autopsy later revealed Vukovich likely had died of head injuries before his car landed upside down and caught on fire, but that didn't soften the blow of the sucker punch felt throughout the racing world. Vukovich would be described more than once in media reports as the Babe Ruth of auto racing — the best, most popular and most colorful driver of all. His withdrawn nature and lack of interest in image and publicity only added to his mystique.

Most fans of the "500" weren't aware of his controversies while coming up through the ranks in California, they only knew him as a dominant champion. They had become acquainted with him through his five races at the Speedway and had grown to like him. How could they not, given his success and the favorable press he received?

Angelo Angelopolous did more than anyone to reveal Vukovich to the public, having featured him in his newspaper columns for four years. After Vukovich qualified for his final race, Angelopolous wrote:

> The capacity for exciting his fellow humans, Bill Vukovich has in overflowing measure. Part of it is the virility of the man, the sparks he sets off. Part of it is the total effort he makes in competition. Part of it is his commanding success. Part of it is his timing. He is a vivid man, both in a race car and afoot.

Following the fatal accident, Angelo praised Vukovich's integrity, courage, physical strength and sense of humor. He called him a "soaring human being" who inspired envy from small-minded people but admiration from everyone else.

The American version of auto racing had not suffered a greater loss to that point, and it had happened so violently and unfairly. Vukovich had been swept up in an unavoidable accident not of his making while leading the race, with no serious challenger. An *Atlanta Constitution* sportswriter, Al Thomy, would later write, "Vuky was driving the perfect race. Others cluttered the highway, and Bill paid."

Respecting the privacy of grieving loved ones was not the norm in that era for news reporters. It wasn't uncommon for photographers to shoot a photo of an accident victim or the child of someone who had just been killed. Several media members gathered in the Thompsons' front yard the evening of the race, seeking comments on the accident. They spoke with Elisian and Boyd, who also rented rooms there during May, much to the chagrin of Lawrence Thompson, who took pride in his well-manicured front yard. Esther did not speak to reporters that evening but made herself available to them the next day while seated on the living room couch.

She had asked Bill to give up racing as far back as 1946, after he suffered injuries in a midget race, but he had pushed back aggressively, and she never spoke of it again. By 1955, she told reporters the day after his death, Bill had lost some of his passion for racing (which he had begun referring to as a "hobby" and as "easy") but had not talked of quitting.

Years later, Billy Jr. also weighed in on his father's mindset approaching his final race.

"I don't think he wanted to run that race," he said in the Sports Century documentary. "I don't think it was a burning desire in him to win three in a row."

Travers, however, said Vukovich's dampened zeal did not affect his driving style, a point supported by Vukovich's performance during his final race.

"I think he lost enthusiasm toward the end there, but it didn't lighten up his foot any," Travers said.

Esther acknowledged a growing sense of impending doom as the years passed, but just 24 hours after losing her husband, she had accepted his fate. Hers, too.

"I'll be feeling fine in a couple of days," she said. "I'll be all right."

Travers and Coon were nearly as devastated as Vukovich's family. They had won two "500s" with him and should have won two more. Propelled by owner Howard Keck's wealth and hands-off management style, they were a spirited and cohesive team that was making history. It's safe to say the three principals in the operation loved one another, although they never would have said so out loud.

Travers reflected on his time with Vukovich nearly 50 years later in a videotaped conversation with Rick Vukovich Amabile, Marlene's son:

"He was one heck of a driver, and he didn't know the meaning of slowing down," Travers said. "When we were leading the race (in 1953), we were giving him the sign ... to slow but he didn't slow. He was one of those guys who had his foot in the thing all the time.

"He was a fun guy to be around. We had lots of fun together."

Their primary version of fun would be called trash talking today. Travers fondly remembered Vukovich making fun of their mechanical prowess. Calling them "butchers," for example.

"He came into the shop in Indianapolis one day and handed me (an ax) and said, 'Hey Smoky, I brought you a new set of tools,'" Travers said.

"I had a badge for being a winning mechanic at Indianapolis. Vuk pinned it to his right shoe and said, 'Hey, Smoky, there's the winning mechanic.'"

Travers also enhanced the anecdote Angelopolous reported regarding their trip to New York to appear on the Firestone television special and the subsequent trip to Broadway.

"See, Vuk, I told you I'd put you on Broadway," Travers said.

Vukovich lifted his right leg to show off the foot he used to avoid lifting from the throttle longer than other drivers and said, "There's what put us on Broadway."

Travers also recalled the '53 race that the team completely dominated, with Vukovich starting on the pole and leading all but five laps. When Vukovich pulled into the Victory Bullpen, completely exhausted, covered with oil and nearly deaf from the noise, Travers shouted, "Vuk, how the hell did you let those five laps slip by?"

"That was you guys' fault, you're too slow in the pits!" Vukovich replied.

All the jokes, however, were a cover for an understood sentiment. "He knew damn well we were the best," Travers said.

One can only imagine, then, the devastation Travers felt when Vukovich lost his life amid the backstretch chaos. He described it to Rick Vukovich Amabile:

"I ran down there, and (Speedway superintendent) Clarence Cagle was there, and the car was upside down on fire and Vuk's arm was sticking out from under it. I asked Cagle, 'What do you think?' He said, 'Jim, he's had it.'

"That was one very, very bitter, bitter pill to swallow."

Travers, though, needed even less time than Esther to shift his focus to the future. Practically no time at all, in fact. Before leaving the track that day he asked McGrath if he would like to replace Vukovich as the driver for the car they were preparing for the 1956 race, the Streamliner. Tested in a wind tunnel at Cal Tech University, it featured a wildly innovative and futuristic design that was more than a decade ahead of its time for aerodynamics and ground effects. McGrath agreed on the spot.

"You've got to be tough," Travers said by way of explanation.

If that seems callous, it reflected the life-goes-on attitude prevalent in racing during that era. Fatalities were so common that those who worked in the industry developed psychological scar tissue to protect their emotions. You either learned to cope with the harsh realities or found another way to make a living. According to Travers, 59 percent of the drivers who raced in the "500" in the fifties eventually died in racing accidents.

"In those days you had to be very, very brave to be a race driver, or a mechanic," he said. He knew from personal experience. He bore scars from once having caught on fire in the pits during a race, forcing him to take off his clothes in front of the grandstand.

"You could get yourself killed monkeying around with any of it," he said.

McGrath, the man immediately chosen to replace Vukovich in the driver's seat, joined the list of fatalities the following November in the final dirt car race of the season in Phoenix after his car flipped. Like Vukovich, he was killed instantly. Like Vukovich, he was 36 years old.

Soon after, Keck quit the auto racing business. It's unknown how much the tragedies and financial losses influenced his decision. What is certain, according to Travers, is that Keck's new bride preferred horses over horsepower. The team that had won two "500s" and should have won two more was finished. Keck sent his secretary to the garage where Travers and Coon were working on the Streamliner and told them to pack their toolboxes.

Keck stuck with racing horses. One of his entries, Ferdinand, won the 1986 Kentucky Derby.

※·※

Vukovich's death numbed the normally joyous and lighthearted atmosphere of the Victory Dinner the evening after race day. Bob Sweikert, who won the race in a pink car that became a feature of the Speedway's museum, addressed what was on all minds when he stepped to the front dais to receive his winner's check of $76,138.63. "I'd gladly

Bob Sweikert, fourth from left, celebrated with his crew after winning the 1955 race but paid tribute to Vukovich at the Victory Dinner the following evening. "I'd gladly give up ever nickel of this, if only Vuky could be here." Racing's cruel reality caught up with Sweikert the following year. (Bob Gates collection)

give up every nickel of this, if only Vuky could be here," he said, struggling to get out the words.

Elisian, a Vukovich understudy who had benefited massively from their relationship, received a sportsmanship trophy for his efforts to aid drivers involved in the accident. He skidded to a stop in the infield and rushed to the aid of Boyd, whose car had flipped over. He tried to help Vukovich as well but was restrained from what would have been a hopeless endeavor. Elisian received a standing ovation upon receiving his honor, then left for the airport before the banquet ended.

Vukovich, who finished 25th, earned the fifth-largest check, $10,833.64, which included $7,500 for having led 50 of the 56 laps he completed.

Two days later, a funeral service was conducted at Conkle Funeral Home before an overflowing crowd. It attracted significant media coverage as reporters sought comment from racing personnel outside.

"Vuky had his own way of getting along with people," Mauri Rose told the *Bee*. "But he earned the admiration and respect of everyone around him."

"He was a great driver — the best in the business, we admit, but I respect the man for the way he took care of his family," added J.C. Agajanian. "He was a family man all the way, and that is something you can't say about most of the drivers."

The presiding minister for the funeral service, Rev. Kenneth E. Thorne, praised him and all the other drivers who had been killed in the "500" as sacrificing heroes.

"We like to think of Bill as being in the same class with those pioneers who gave their lives that we might have something worthwhile," Thorne said. "We owe a great debt to the Speedway and those men who constantly risk their lives there. Progress goes on. Life goes on and others will risk their lives in the future.

"... William Vukovich, like so many other greats, gave his life in doing something which would help mankind."

That likely was of small comfort to Esther and Mike Vukovich, who sat in a private room off to the side during the service. They flew with Vukovich's body the following morning to Fresno, where another service was conducted on Saturday. An estimated 2,000 people attended, some forced to stand outside on the sidewalk in front of the Free Evangelical Lutheran Cross Church. Hundreds of floral arrangements, shaped like steering wheels, tires, checkered flags and racing ovals, filled the chapel. Following the service, a police motorcycle unit led a mile-long procession to Belmont Memorial Park for the graveside service and burial.

Fate ultimately took a horrible toll on the 1955 "500" starting field. Jerry Hoyt, the unlikely polesitter, was killed in a sprint car race in Oklahoma City in July, followed by McGrath in November. Walt Faulkner died the following year after he crashed while qualifying for a stock car event in Vallejo, Calif. Tony Bettenhausen died while testing a car at the Speedway in 1961.

Thus, five of the top seven qualifiers for the '55 race were killed in action within six years. In all, sixteen of the thirty-three drivers would die in racing accidents. That list doesn't include Manny Ayulo, who had been killed in practice for the race or Andy Linden, who suffered a brain injury in a 1957 race that ended his career. It also omitted the cruelly ill-fated Niday, who lost a leg in a motorcycle accident shortly after graduating from high school, drove with a prosthetic leg, and suffered serious injuries and burns resulting from an accident on his 170th lap of the '55 race and was hospitalized for 67 days. He died from a heart attack after being thrown from a vintage open wheeler at age 73 in 1988.

In June of 1955, a driver in the 24 Hours of Lemans race in France, Pierre Levegh, lost control of his car and killed an untold number of spectators — 83 according to some reports, perhaps more. Several European countries banned auto racing as a result, and an Oregon senator, Richard Neuberger, called for the same to happen in the United States. Popular evangelist Billy Graham joined the crusade. The sport's sanctioning body, the American Automobile Association, announced it would cease operations at the end of the year, which led to the formation of the Temporary Emergency Committee in Indianapolis to find ways to preserve and improve the sport. The United States Auto Club replaced the AAA and racing survived — barely.

Racing journalists assumed a defensive posture against the threats, treating the fatalities as an unfortunate cost of doing business. Bill Fox, *The Indianapolis News* sports editor and lead columnist, pointed out in May of 1956 that "only four of those who started last year's race are dead." As if it was no big deal. Perhaps for that era it wasn't.

A columnist for *The Indianapolis Times*, Bill Eggert, claimed racing in the "500" was safer than driving on the nation's highways, offering statistics to back his argument. He also conjured a creative comparison to boxing.

"An ex-race driver is either dead or alive, not half groggy like some ex-fighters," he wrote.

Oscar Fraley, a United Press International writer who later gained acclaim as the co-author of the book, "The Untouchables," which became the basis for a popular television series, was more tolerant of opposing opinions but couldn't resist the race's everlasting appeal:

You can understand those sentiments. On Friday I was at a dinner with Vuky. On Monday I was sick when he got it. Right then I didn't believe I'd ever come back to the 500.

But I will.

It draws you like a magnet. Because it provides the most dramatic moments in sports.

＊-＊

Bill Vukovich remained a presence at the Speedway for decades to follow. His success, unique persona, and the horrific manner in which he lost his life were too dramatic to be forgotten quickly.

The details of the backstretch accident were still a topic of discussion in the sixties. Ward, who won the "500" in 1959 and '62, described it to a *News* reporter in '63:

"Billy was a victim of circumstances. There was nothing he could do to avoid it. My front axle broke, and I hit the outside retaining wall, facing oncoming traffic. Al Keller was the first car to avoid me, and he lost control. He ran into Johnny Boyd and Boyd's car wound up in line with Vuky's car.

"I got a bruised arm and a cut nose, but 10 days later I was back racing at Milwaukee."

Ward recalled it again for the Sports Century documentary more than 35 years later:

"I still blame myself for not having the good judgment to bring that car in off the race track and put it in the garage, because that car is what caused the accident and we lost one of the truly great people in the universe in Bill Vukovich. Every time I think about it, I still get upset."

Ward said, however, that Eli Vukovich had told him Bill would have been angry if he retired from racing because of his unintended role in the accident.

"So, I didn't, and I won two," Ward said, smiling.

Fans haven't forgotten Vukovich, either. The photograph on the back cover of this book, taken in his garage after his victory in 1954 (not '53 as many people assume) remains the best seller in the Speedway's photo shop. Although taken in a moment of glory, it seems to capture his career in one click of the shutter.

Most of all, however, his family kept his name alive. Racing coursed through the Vukovich bloodlines, drawing them "like a magnet" to the most dangerous game.

In August of 1955, less than three months after his brother's death, Eli announced he would enter the '56 race despite never having raced a championship car. He arrived at the track early in May, insisting he would only accept a ride in a "good car" because Bill had told him to "stay out of those clunkers." The *Star* ran a photo of him standing in the garage area in its May 2 edition, but no offers were forthcoming. It wouldn't have made sense for an owner to entrust a "good car" to a driver with no relevant experience no matter what his last name happened to be.

Although Eli couldn't find a spot in the field, Vukovich's car did. Incredibly, it was restored and driven in the '56 race by Jim Rathmann. In fact, he set a one-lap record of 146.033 and a four-lap record of 145.120 early on the first day of qualifications, although he wound up starting third. The *News* and *Bee* both referred to it as a "Death Car" in headlines. Rathmann led three laps but dropped out after 175 laps with engine failure and finished 20th.

Esther and her children skipped the race. They stayed in Fresno, where on May 30 an 11-foot statue of Bill was unveiled in front of the Fresno Memorial Auditorium. Billy Jr. and Marlene pulled the drawstring to remove the canvas covering before a crowd of about 300, including city and county officials and their teary-eyed mother.

Esther took Marlene to the Speedway two weeks later, on June 15, for a private experience. Angelopolous had the exclusive story in the *News* of their visit, which was arranged by Clarence Cagle. Esther drove Marlene around the track, accompanied by Dorcas Thompson and her daughter, Susie. Billy Jr. was left at home because his undefeated Little League team was in the midst of a pennant race.

Esther said her daughter "wanted to get something settled in her mind."

Earl Motter, above, hoped to qualify for the "500" in 1959 but crashed in practice. (IMS Photos)

Motter and Esther, left, married in 1958 but later divorced. She happily retreated to her family in Fresno. (Courtesy Joe Young)

Two days later, Sweikert, who won the race Vukovich should have won, lost his life in a sprint car race in Salem, Ind. under circumstances eerily similar to Vukovich's accident. Sweikert's right rear wheel clipped a steel beam jutting from the outside wall, causing his car to flip over the wall, crash through a photographer's stand and land 100 feet down an embankment in a weed patch and catch on fire. Just 30 years old, he was pronounced dead of head injuries at the hospital. His wife was at the track. His children, three of them, were at home. His funeral service was conducted at Conkle and his body flown to Hayward, Calif. for burial.

Esther and her children returned to the Speedway for the 1957 race. Billy Jr., then 13, was asked if he had any interest in becoming a race driver. He had replied negatively in the past, but this time he hedged: "A little." He made newspaper headlines for picking Jimmy Bryan to win that year's race. Bryan was called into the garage to meet Billy and posed for a photo with him. Another photo of Billy Jr. with Esther and Speedway owner Tony Hulman watching practice from behind a chain link fence appeared in newspapers throughout the county.

Bill Jr.'s prediction wasn't far off. Bryan finished third in the "500" that year and won it in '58. But racing's relentless threat caught up with him as well. He was killed at the Langhorne (Pa.) Speedway in 1960.

Racing maintained a grip on Esther, too. After all, it had provided her with a community of friends and so many thrills despite the constant anxiety. Perhaps her quest to be "all right" again and regain something resembling her former life was what led her to marry one of Bill's best friends from the racing world, Earl Motter. She and Bill had shared many moments off the track with Motter and his first wife, but the Motters had divorced.

Motter announced their engagement at the Speedway in May of 1958 and photos ran in newspapers throughout the country of them smiling and showing off her ring. He no doubt reminded Esther of Bill in some ways. A World War II veteran, he had paid his dues with Bill on the midget and sprint car circuits and had some success. His most notable victory was in the Bill Vukovich Memorial Race in Fresno in 1956. His collar was as blue as Bill's, too. He worked as a mechanic and performed body repairs away from racing.

Unlike Bill, however, he couldn't find success at the Speedway. He passed his rookie test in 1958 but failed to land a ride to attempt to qualify. He got a ride in '59 but crashed during practice and suffered a minor neck injury, ending that dream.

The marriage crashed as well. Earl and Esther married in October of '58 and divorced in June of 1966. The relationship was over well before that, however. Esther, who filed, testified that Motter "resented" Marlene and Billy Jr., argued with her constantly, and had refused to escort her down the church aisle when her son was married in March of '63.

Esther remained a presence at the Speedway into the seventies, working as a hostess in the Champion Spark Plug hospitality suite beneath the main grandstand at the Speedway. A hangout for former and current drivers, it enabled her to maintain many of the friendships she had established in the racing world. She no longer stayed with Dorcas Thompson — who never attended another race after 1955 according to her grandson, Greg — renting a room instead with Virgil and Dorothy Sharp in their modest 900-square foot home within a mile of the Speedway's main gate.

Marlene made return trips to the Speedway as well. A wire service photo of her with five-year-old daughter Jackie ran in newspapers in 1967, further evidence of the staying power of Bill Vukovich's legend. That also was the year another driver, Parnelli Jones, finally surpassed him for prize money for leading the most laps. It took 12 years. Jones, the 1963 winner who was competing in his seventh and final "500," led 171 laps of the '67 race before he was forced out by a broken transmission bearing three laps from the finish.

Vukovich's legacy was further refueled in 1968 when Billy Jr. made his racing debut at the Speedway. Junior inherited much of Dad's talent and reticent personality but not his extreme aggression. That's understandable, given that he had grown up in a much more comfortable and stable environment than the extreme poverty and tragedy of Bill

Sr.'s childhood. Junior wanted to make his living from racing but also wanted to live a long life.

Besides, technological advancements were gradually homogenizing the cars so that a driver's skill was becoming less of a factor in the winning equation. Not lifting from the throttle in turns was no longer the sharp dividing line between winner and also-ran it once had been.

Whereas Vukovich Sr. had been compared to Babe Ruth, Billy Jr. was equated to silent film star Rudolf Valentino because of his handsome features and cool, quiet demeanor. He wasn't going to put his life in danger by trying to live up to Dad's reputation.

"Racing to my father was a way of making a buck," he said in the Sports Century documentary. "I felt the same way."

Still, at age 24, he made a splash in the 1968 "500" by finishing seventh and winning Rookie of the Year honors. He finished second in 1973 (29 seconds behind winner Gordon Johncock), third in '74 and sixth in '75. He raced in 12 "500s" overall, with six top 10 finishes, and won one championship car event, a 125-mile race in Michigan in 1973.

He failed to qualify in his last three attempts at the Speedway and retired in 1983. He was inducted into the National Midget Auto Racing Hall of Fame in 1998.

His father's ghost accompanied him throughout his career. It provided a natural story angle for the media when he first qualified at Indianapolis, 13 years after the '55 race, but was not a comfortable topic for him to discuss.

"Don't get me wrong, I'm very proud of what my father accomplished," he said. "But I've won a lot of races myself and that was me sitting behind the wheel, not my father."

He described himself as a "safety-first" driver, acknowledged he wasn't capable of winning as a rookie, and even at that early stage of his racing career was growing weary of it all. "This isn't fun anymore," he said. "...when you get into this competition and this kind of speed, there is danger involved. No, I wouldn't say I really enjoy it now."

He would have finished even better than seventh as a rookie if not for two bad breaks. He was black flagged and forced to pull off the track after twenty laps because race officials thought he was leaking oil. He

Vukovich was inducted into the Auto Racing Hall of Fame during a ceremony at the Indianapolis 500 Oldtimers Club dinner in May of 1972. Bill Jr. and Esther accepted the honor on his behalf. The hall of fame was later renamed the Indianapolis Motor Speedway Hall of Fame and is part of the IMS Museum. (IMS Photo)

wasn't, and was allowed back in the race, but lost precious time. On the 126th lap he bumped wheels with Mel Kenyon and spun out in the fourth turn. He avoided contact with the wall and got his car rolling again but arrived at a nearly empty pit because his crew members, thinking he was out of the race, were running toward the scene of his spin. He returned to the race for a few laps to give them time to get back to their pit, and then stopped again for new tires.

He said he would have finished third without those delays. Unlike his father, he took it easy at the start of the race to avoid an accident. But much like his father he downplayed both his performance and the event.

"The race wasn't as tough as I thought it would be," he said.

It surely was plenty tough on his mother, however. "I think she's just glad it's over," he said.

His car owner, Agajanian, was pleased with Junior's careful performance, which provided valuable experience. "We're going to keep coming back here, and in two or three years, Bill will win here," he said.

Bill Jr. got fed up and quit racing — all forms of it — for a stretch during the 1970 season but soon realized he had no better options. He regained some of his enthusiasm in 1971, by which time he had accepted his place as a legend's son.

"I used to think, 'Why do people always talk to me about my dad?'" he told Dick Mittman of the *News*. "But I guess people root for me because of my dad. If Babe Ruth had a son and the kid played baseball, I know I'd root for him because he was Babe Ruth's son."

Vukovich Jr. also gained prominence for other athletic talents. The former Little League all-star was a talented golfer as well. He won the golf outing for drivers, mechanics, and race officials at the Speedway course multiple times, shooting in the low- to mid-seventies, and was a frequent celebrity participant in charity events. There had been no mention of Bill Vukovich Sr. having the slightest interest in such a genteel sport as golf, but his more careful son was well-suited for it.

→-←

Billy Vukovich III followed his father's path as the "500's" Rookie of the Year, winning the honor in 1988. (Bob Gates collection)

A third William John Vukovich entered the world on Aug. 31, 1963, born to Bill Jr. and Joyce in Fresno while his father was busy establishing himself as a leading sprint and midget racer in California.

Mom and Dad didn't want him to race. What parents would encourage their son to enter a profession so dangerous when the original Bill Vukovich was Exhibit 1A? But then how could they forbid him to do what his father and grandfather had done?

"My dad never wanted me to race," Billy III said in 1984. "Neither did my mom. My dad told me my chances of going to Indy were a million to one."

He beat the odds with talent, although bloodlines and professional mentoring certainly were benefits. He began his racing career after graduating from high school but didn't receive undue favors. He won the United States Auto Club supermodified championship in 1987 by winning 12 of the 17 events, including seven in a row. He won Rookie of the Year honors for the "500" in 1988 when, at age 22, he started 23rd and finished 14th, following the groove laid down by his father 20 years earlier.

He also repeated his father's experience with the media. Virtually every story about Billy III made an obligatory reference to Bill Vukovich dying in the 1955 race while going for his third consecutive victory. For the family, it was a tragedy that would not go away. But Billy III loved his profession, more than his father had. He was a better driver, too — at least in his father's opinion.

"I just think he has more natural ability," Bill Jr. said.

That didn't make it any easier for the middle Bill Vukovich. He openly acknowledged the anxiety he felt when his son raced, often stating he wished Billy III had chosen a safer profession. Although closely involved in his son's preparation for races he rarely watched him in competition, preferring to hide away in the garage area or roam amid the motor homes while listening to the radio broadcast.

Billy III finished 12th in the 1989 "500" and 24th in '90. The month did not go well for him that year. Two minutes before the track closed on May 7, he lost control and hit the wall exiting the first turn. He suffered a concussion, was hospitalized overnight for observation, and cleared to drive a few days later. His car wasn't ready until the 14th and was never quite right for the race. Engine failure forced him out after 102 laps.

At a midget race in August of that year, he accepted a plaque that recognized Bill Vukovich Sr. as an inductee into the Midget Racing Hall of Fame.

"I never knew my grandfather," he said. "I was born eight years after he was killed, but I am proud to be mentioned with him."

He and his grandfather became forever fatally linked on Nov. 25, when he was killed during practice for a sprint car race at the Mesa Mann Raceway in Bakersfield, Calif. The cause of the accident, in which he slammed nearly head-on into the third-turn wall, was never determined.

His parents, who were living in Indianapolis at the time, flew back to bury their son. Their worst fears were realized as another chapter was added to the family's tragic history. John Vukovich had committed suicide in 1932, three days after his brother died and, reportedly, after foreclosure proceedings had been initiated on his farm. Bill perished in a racing accident in 1955. And now Bill's grandson, just 27 years old, had lost his life in another accident.

Bill Jr. and Joyce, of course, never got over it. They lived out their lives as normally as possible, quietly and with aching hearts, living alternately in Fresno and Indianapolis.

Bill Jr. rarely spoke of his cruel fate — losing both his father and son to racing accidents — but summarized it vividly for the Sports Century

The Bill Vukovich Memorial in Fresno, unveiled in 1956. (Photo by Mike Garabedian)

documentary:

"I think about Billy every day. I think about my dad every day. I haven't come to terms with either one of 'em's death and probably never will.

"There's not going to be any more Vukoviches in a race car and I'm glad of that. That suits me just fine."

Vukovich Amabile saw the impact Billy III's death had on Bill Jr.

"It ruined his life when Billy died," he said.

Joyce offered her thoughts in 2019 to Indianapolis radio personality Jake Query, the third-turn reporter for the Speedway radio network's coverage of the "500," after they had a chance meeting at the airport in Austin, Tex.

"I told (Billy), this is a dangerous sport," she said. "I believe you bring a child into this world, you open your hands, and you let them fly."

Bill Vukovich Jr. lived to be 79 years old. Unlike his father and son, he survived his racing career, but he couldn't outlast his own terrible fate. He suffered from dementia in his later years before passing away on Aug. 20, 2023. He and Joyce had moved back to Fresno to be closer to friends and family members but when Joyce became ill earlier that summer and had to be hospitalized her husband was inadvertently left alone in their home for four days without care. He survived on ice cream and soda before being moved into a care facility, where he soon passed.

By then, it was for the best.

"He was going to be really miserable," said longtime friend Mike Garabedian. "Joyce couldn't take care of him at that point."

Joyce at least was able to attend his funeral services — private and public — despite her severely declining health.

Esther lived out her life in Fresno, residing most of those years with Marlene, her daughter; Marlene's husband, Ralph Amabile; and their children, Jackie and Rick. She worked in a department store in her later years before dying of an aneurysm at age 62.

"She was happier after her divorce than when she was married," Joyce said before becoming ill. "She had her daughter and grandchildren and kept busy. I would say her life was fine."

The judge at Esther's divorce hearing asked if she wanted to reclaim Vukovich as her legal last name but she declined. Jackie, however, saw to it that the name on her tombstone, placed next to Bill's, was "Esther Vukovich."

Marlene also died of an aneurysm, in 2009 at age 68.

Rick Amabile did not legally change his name but began going by Rick Vukovich Amabile in 1993. He was writing racing guides by then and realized that since Billy III's death nobody was left to carry on the Vukovich family name. It was his way of keeping it alive, at least within the racing world.

The Vukovich family legacy, however, will forever be part of Fresno. The statue of Bill Sr. that was unveiled the weekend of the "500" in 1956, when Marlene and Bill Jr. pulled the cord to remove the canvas covering, was moved from Memorial Auditorium to Selland Arena after the newer facility was completed in 1966. The Auditorium and Selland are still standing but Save Mart Center has become the city's primary sports and concert venue since opening in 2003, leaving the statue in a less prominent location.

Bill and Esther are reunited in the Belmont Memorial Park cemetery in Fresno.
(Photo courtesy Belmont Memorial Park)

Bill Vukovich Sr. was an original inductee into the Fresno Athletic Hall of Fame when it opened in 1959. He later was joined by his son and grandson. The organization lacked sufficient funds to keep its museum open, however, and the plaques were moved to Fresno City Hall. The hall of fame still exists as a website and is hoping to reopen at the Save Mart Center.

A historical marker also was installed outside city hall on June 8, 2019, honoring all three of the racing Vukoviches. A brief ceremony was conducted with Bill Jr. and Joyce in attendance and the mayor declared it Vukovich Day. The marker later was moved next to the statue outside Selland Arena.

The three Bills and their families have earned every bit of recognition they have received, paying for it many times over with heartbreak. They are all together again, most of them anyway, in the Belmont Memorial Park cemetery. Bill Sr.'s parents are buried there, identified by their original last name of Vucurovich. Bill and Esther are side by side again. Marlene, Bill Jr., and Billy III are nearby.

They all contributed to a legend that will forever be etched in racing lore — remembered for its glory, its tragedies and all of those ifs.

Acknowledgements

I can't be certain why this book wasn't published as scheduled in 1960 while Angelo Angelopolous was alive. But I think I know the primary reason nobody took on the project after he passed away. It needed a lot of work. Painstaking, dreary, hour-inhaling work.

The manuscript, littered with scrawled edits, was a powerful repellant all its own. That's why the first person deserving of thanks for helping revive Angelo's abandoned work is my wife, Faith. She retyped his words — every one of them, including the ones he had crossed out — into a laptop to initiate the editing process. That was more than anyone else had dared attempt for more than 60 years. She also was a diligent proofreader, crucial to the metamorphosis from unfinished manuscript to published book.

Photographer Joe Young, a former colleague of Angelo's for *The Indianapolis News*, worked his magic to help acquire photographs. He also accompanied me to the Indiana Historical Society and Marion County Library to search for more. Actually, he did more than accompany me. He drove. I hope I can navigate the traffic on I-465 as well as he does after I've turned 90.

Rick Vukovich Amabile, Bill's grandson, went to the trouble of mailing a DVD of an interview he conducted with Jim Travers and provided other background information.

Another Fresno resident, Mike Garabedian, was a fountain of information and more than generous in providing photos from his collection. He even went to the trouble of taking a few himself.

206 ● VUKOVICH: THE MAN WHO WOULDN'T LIFT

Kendra Wilson, head of the Indianapolis Motor Speedway Museum's photo department, was a congenial and knowledgeable professional who helped execute the loan of Vukovich photos for this book. Thanks also to Joe Skibinski, the Speedway's photo archivist, for his cooperation. I paid for their photos, sure, but they made the process as seamless as possible.

Bob Gates, author of "Vukovich: An Inspiring Story of American Achievement," could have resented another effort to publish a book on the same subject he explored 20 years ago but he couldn't have been more helpful. He loaned photos, provided valuable background information, and connected me with other sources. He displayed great sportsmanship and is a credit to the auto racing fraternity.

Bob put me in touch with Bonnie Bruhn, who owns and lives in the house where Bill and Esther Vukovich stayed when in Indianapolis. She is a gracious host who has carried on the house's rich tradition by renting rooms to race fans. She allowed me to take a photograph of her home for use in the book and provided background information about her home's history.

Employees of the Belmont Memorial Park Cemetery in Fresno went to the trouble to take and transmit photographs of grave markers. Dr. Warrick L. Barrett, whose photos are included on the cemetery's website, also shared what he had taken. Dr. Barrett has appeared and reappeared in my life over the past 40 years for a variety of reasons and in various locations and shines every time.

Scott Johnston, Producer and Program Coordinator for 93.5 and 107.5 The Fan Radio, sent a recording of the station's broadcast of the 1955 race for review. Thanks also to his supervisor, David Wood, for granting permission. Listening to the fateful broadcast, one couldn't help but hope for the miracle of a different outcome.

Susan Loman, widow of the inaugural winner of Arlington High School's Angelo Angelopolous Mental Attitude Award, took time late on a Sunday evening to dig through a box of her late husband Steve's memorabilia. She provided a photo and contact information for Steve's best friend, Steve Wolkoff, who also was generous with his time and knowledge.

Many others were cooperative when contacted — in some cases as far back as 15 years ago — for information, a photograph or a phone number. They include Joyce Vukovich, Greg Thompson, Donald Davidson, Dick Mittman, Jimmie Angelopolous, Joann Angelopolous, Bob Doeppers, Curt Cavin, Jake Query, Graham Honaker and Lyle Mannweiler. Apologies to anyone I might have missed.

None of these people would have been asked for help, however, if not for Pete Kirles, longtime owner of Kirles Jewelers in Indianapolis. Angelo's nephew and closest living relative, Pete had the good sense not to throw out the yellowing manuscript buried in his closet for so many decades. He offered it up without hesitation once I found him and learned of it and allowed me to edit without interference. More than anyone, he's responsible for this book's long overdue birth. He's made his uncle proud.

Mark Montieth

February, 2024

Also from Halfcourt Press

Reborn: The Pacers and the Return of Pro Basketball to Indianapolis is the riveting story of the formation and formative years of the Indiana Pacers, who opened for business in 1967 and awakened a slumbering city. It traces the events that enabled Indianapolis to become a charter member of the American Basketball Association and reveals the diligent effort, exceptional talent and dumb luck that got the team up and running – and winning – in two electrifying and tumultuous seasons.

Available at Amazon.com and through www.markmontieth.com.